Everything is Opportunity

Creating your future

Written By: Shane L. Freeman

1-1-2019

Printed in the US

Through CreateSpace Independent Publishing Platform

This book is dedicated to my sons.

They keep me accountable and push me to refine myself constantly.

Table of Contents

Chapter

PREFACE

I'm not here to be the hype man. I'm actually the quiet guy in the crowd. I only speak when I feel the need to deliver pertinent information. Anyone can give you an answer to your question. Anyone can tell you what the result will be if you listen to their advice. There is a difference between a result and a solution. I can say, "You just gotta think positive man!" Or maybe, "Hustle harder!" Any cliché pump up the crowd type quote that the masses copy and share, repost and retweet. Many people have answers to all the questions out there, but very few have solutions.

We need a specific way. A map. It's easy to pump up a crowd with a motivational speech, but if you aren't charting a path the hype is useless. This book is a practical guide loaded with applicable solutions to real life problems and issues. We live in a fast-paced world and it's not slowing down anytime soon. The words within give guidance on how to take control over the time we do have and focus our attention and intentions in the directions which will create the life you desire. I'm not asking for a follow **#Freeway_Child**. I am giving you my truth. I am laying out what I know has saved my life. Allow this work to provide you with the solutions, a path, an alternate course, and above all an abundance of opportunities.

CHAPTER 1

WHAT'S BROKE?

Let's not waste any time. This is a short book, so we need to get down to the nitty-gritty at once. I ask you, "What's broke?" is it the system, is it external, is it banking institutions, is it the government, is it the school system, the global markets, the economy, politics, religion, family, friendships? Are you walking around saying aloud and telling others, "I'm broke"? What exactly do you see as the problem you're facing? You might want to start taking notes at this point, because from here on out we have a lot of details to cover in a short amount of time.

God forbid you have lost it all and you're on your last leg when this book crossed your path. I would like to propose you give thanks to the unlikely event that you are reading this book, even if having nothing, but this material in your possession. My plan is for this information to be transformational. Hopefully for the better. This is practical advice that I have applied in my own life and I can say unequivocally I am doing better now than ever.

I say that reading this book is an unlikely event, not because I lack confidence in the significance within it. I use the word unlikely in referring to the chance that I would have written it in the first place. Considering the fact that just six years ago, I was headed nowhere fast, this book was unlikely to arise. A term coined in the recovery community which could have summed up my potential as, "Jails, institutions, and death." I was flat ass broke! Not a dollar to my name. I felt as if the system had failed me. I felt that I had failed my family. I was uncertain of my God. I hadn't much more hope than a prayer. I didn't believe with all my being that I was ever going to succeed. I felt like a failure and lashed out at anyone with a, "Maybe you should" suggestion.

The prognosis was grim, I thought the best I could do with my life was a low skill, low pay, revolving door type job. I would be a clerk of some type for life and believe me I tried on many of those shoes. The job wouldn't matter anyway because my attitude in life could have been graded with an F. For many years, I contemplated just giving up on trying to make something of myself and going to live under a bridge. These were serious thoughts for many lonely nights. I never got to the point of suicide, but some of my friends chose that way out. Three to count correctly, and when you think of how few friends one generally has, 3 becomes an astronomical number.

The reason I highlight these low parts of my life is to let you know that I can relate to your troubles. I've been in many precarious situations myself. I'm not trying to go toe-to-toe with you and compare our evils. Just know that when I speak of the brutal realities and pitfalls of life, I speak from experience. I'm very well versed in the variations of hopelessness; addiction, abuse, poverty, ignorance, failure, debt, homelessness, you name it. Through life experience and developmental research, I have lived through, studied, and overcome these conditions. I understand how one can get themselves into these circumstances and I know what it takes to get out of them all first hand.

It's hard to think of some good when we are buried in bad circumstances, surrounded by negative energy, and bombarded with distraction. Hope can be the furthest thing from our minds. Even when we try to be hopeful, we find our mental conditioning mocking us internally. Our mind won't let us conceive the notion of a positive outcome when we have told it repeatedly how nothing good ever happens. Like were trapped in a box, inescapable. One bill after another, bad break ups, disgruntled employer, health problems, family problems, most of us are likely to have experienced these. They all add up, and after a while, we become hostile and negative ourselves. It's not like we were born pissed off. Although it appears we come into this world pretty scared, crying, and screaming. The plan is to learn from the pains and adapt to our environment. In the end, we want to live in comfort, have purpose, be loved, and leave peacefully. They say the road to heaven is a path through hell. If you're in a low place, going through a lonely time, or some of life's speed bumps, just hang tight, or rejoice. There are lessons abound.

EMOTIONAL TRANCES

I'm reminded of the story of how I lost my first tooth. I was in the first grade and it was recess, the most celebrated part of the day for a child. However, during this time I was troubled by a bully on the playground and a stubborn loose tooth. I don't recall which caused more torture, my fear of all the pain of losing a tooth, or my fear of the bully throwing me around. Anyhow while running after him he head-bunted me in the mouth knocking out my tooth. First the impact should have sent me to the teacher bawling with tears. I grabbed that tooth out of my mouth and my anger and pain transformed into laughter and adulation. A revolution of mind came over me, I ecstatically thanked the boy for knocking out my tooth. This kind of caught him off guard because I'm sure he thought he was about to be in big trouble. He was looking at me skeptically with this half-smile blank stare like, "Is this real life?"

So, what does that have to do with desperation, or pain, brokenness, poverty, homelessness, or opportunity? Well, looking back at it that little incident has within it quite the life lesson. I was stuck in an *emotional trance*. My time, energy, and mental faculties were consumed with "what if's". All the fear, and anger, hostility, animosity and resentment I had for the boy was relinquished in a second. On the other side of that fear and pain was a blessing in disguise. No more was I troubled by that wiggly tooth and no more was a troubled by that intimidating bully. The experience of the pain, and of the fear, defeated them.

If this story didn't quite make the connection for you between pain and blessing let me highlight one more personal story. This Moment became the turning point in my life. Well, it was one very distinct turning point anyway.

The Story begins with me and three friends. We all chose to link up and get drinks for the night in the downtown district of our city. A couple of us were tired of paying the premium drink prices at the clubs so we decided I would drive us to the gas station for a good ole six pack. Upon arriving back downtown I entered a bustling parking lot. We all heard this loud "Clink Clank" sound and concurred that someone must have thrown a bottle of beer at the truck. So, I immediately reversed and gave chase to the presumed guilty party. I was caught in another *emotional trance*, fueled by alcohol, and social contracts. The concoction sparked a cascade of spontaneous uncontrolled decisions. We weaved in and out of traffic giving chase across town. Some of the parties were hanging out the window yelling intimidating banter. After 10 minutes, we decided to call off the chase and head back to the bar. Just then I sped past a police van with one of the guys still sitting on the window sill. Needless to say, he began his pursuit. Long story short, the people being chased had called the police. Come to find out in court and during the revolutionary insight years later, they were innocent. A few of us bailed out and ran on foot. I was caught and ended up facing 7 years in prison for OWI 2 and felony eluding. With one son, and one on the way, my world came crashing down. I decided obviously, I better straighten up, but I didn't know how. After having tried to sober up in the past I was finally able to get it right. The right amount of incentives, pains, and turmoil allowed for the course correction. Many years of trial and error would lead me down a path of self-education and discovery.

Now let me fast-forward three years from that incident. That chaotic moment of my life was the furthest thing from my mind. I was standing on a balcony downtown overlooking that same parking lot where it all started. I just happened to be there visiting my friend at his apartment. I stepped outside to get some fresh air and take in the view. All the sudden I hear, "Clink Clank" and was transported back in time. I look down and to my surprise I see a car had just entered the lot across the street passing over a metal grate type storm drain. It was the exact same driveway I entered on that fateful night. "Clink Clank", the sound resonated in my mind. I knew right then the entire incident was inspired by an illusion. An assumption, a conviction, a false belief changed my life in an instant.

What I perceived as the worst consequence, and one of my worst acts to date, was actually the catalyst for magnificent change. Jail time, probation, thousands of dollars in fines, thousands of dollars lost in potential earned income, and the loss of my license to drive for 6 years, loss of friendships, loss of love, and ever-increasing insecurity almost defeated me. I was morally tainted, emotionally depleted, and physically exhausted. I wanted a way out so bad, but couldn't dig my way out of the ditch, I just kept digging down. You see I had been praying for years to no avail. In hindsight however, my prayers were being answered. It was just a matter of time. For everything there is a season.

Finally, a window of opportunity burst wide open. We people are a hard-headed lot. Generally, it takes a life or death situation to incite real change. Even after facing death we can find ourselves resuming our once sworn off life choices. Our mind has ways of deceiving us, our vices are deceptive, and our tolerance for pain increases. The more we are exposed to certain types of pain, the more we become accustomed to them. This contributes to our baffling behaviors.

What I want you to take away from these two illustrations is the fact that pleasures in life are complementary to the pain we experience. I know it may not seem that way, but I assure you it is a matter of perspective. It's a universal law of nature that orders a natural balance. When you consider any aspect of life you must recognize the existence of complementary opposites; pain and pleasure, hot and cold, light and dark, up and down. All these things appear separate from each other, but they are intimately tied together. Woven in the fabric of creation is an unavoidable entanglement which inexplicably ties us all together. We are all bound through action and consequence. Our thoughts, words, and deeds not only mold our reality, but flow to and from us, our family, and society. We all must recognize the pains in life as necessary elements to our growth. We need to fall to walk, it's part of the process.

We all cause pain. We all get hurt. I'm not saying that pain isn't real. All I'm saying is that pain is necessary. I know there are a lot of instances in life that we could say, "That didn't have to happen." I urge you to be open to the idea that in this life, in this world, on this journey, the appearance of pain is ultimately an illusion. Everything happens for a reason. I know it sounds cliché, but there is a deeper meaning to it. That reason may be self-imposed and the way it played out you cannot see yet. I suspect we will find no one was truly hurt in the end. Maybe the more painful part is the torture we put ourselves through thinking about the pain. How it might feel to experience whatever it may be.

SEEING THROUGH THE PAIN

So how do we break through and see the pain for what it really is? The answer to this question is multi-faceted and perhaps personal to the extent that only you can uncover the truths. Different pains vary and the complexities of issues that surround them vary more extensively. However, they are all similar in the fact that they cause us mental agony. This anxiety, stress, or burden upon our minds creates the real suffering in life. How well we come to terms with the psychological effects of pain is the primary determining factor of our healing. It's not the injury itself that we fear; it is our thinking about the pain where fear arises.

I want you to try a little exercise. Either you can take 30 minutes at the end of this chapter or you can make notes over the next 30 days. Either method or both will be beneficial. What I want you to do is think back on some of the painful moments in your history or observe them as they appear. Whether you experienced physical pain or emotional pain doesn't matter. What we are going to do is look at this occurrence as an objective bystander. I want you to analyze these incidents from the outside with these questions in mind.

1. Was it my fault?

    In this question, be thorough and honest. Put
    yourself up on the stand and ask the question under
    presumed penalty of perjury. Were you seeking
    something for personal gain? Were your actions
    careless? Was it the result of an accumulation of
    wrong decisions? Were you uninformed? These are
    prompts that may help you when delving into this
    realm. Understand that in this universe there are
    laws, one of them being cause and effect. It all
    strings together in some way.

2. Is this my pain or someone else's?

    Many times in life we will carry pain with us that is
    not ours to carry. What I mean is that it is someone
    else's problem that we have taken on as our own.
    We are a communal species, so it is in our nature to
    feel for others. To a degree this is healthy,
    productive, and good. However, many people drive
    themselves insane or carry high levels of stress
    worrying about someone else's problem. In the
    interest of being succinct let's just simplify the
    answer with a mine or not mine.

3. Is it justifiable?

    Can you find reason within yourself as to why this
    incident may have occurred? This is much easier to

do in retrospect as we cannot make out the future as clearly as we can see the past. My suggestion for you is this, if you can understand why the pain happened, then you have seen what you needed to see, and you can thank that pain, and let it go. If you cannot find any justification for it, which I'm sure you have searched far and wide, then it is not meant to be justified. Some things in life are meant not to be understood and through that confusion we grow where needed. So, if it cannot be justified, then stress no longer, for all the dwelling will not bring you to peace. Thank this confusion for allowing you to grow and let it go. In fact, letting it go for the simple reason of your own peace of mind may have been the lesson all along.

The reason I want to address these issues is to try and demonstrate that nothing outside of you is broken. What we have instead is a fragmented understanding of reality. Putting the pieces together in a way that you can identify with will help your understanding to become whole, which in turn lays to rest some of the stress and anxiety you might feel. Letting go of the anguish that old pains have plagued us with, and objectively observing new hurtful incidents is freeing. This process helps you unclutter the mind. The goal is to eliminate any negative preconceived notions (unwarranted fears) we may have in our normal daily lives. The building up of thoughts is what makes us. So, if we're constantly thinking about the negative outcomes then we will continue to suffer. Either in our mind by torture or our bodies by action and consequence, the unwanted results will continue. Not even to mention the direct correlation between thought and physical health. To this respect there is a mountain of evidence and countless books which explain the detrimental effects of stress on the body. What I truly want to emphasize is that true pain exists in the mind. It is not some external event or occurrence. You might think, "Ouch", as you hit your hand with a hammer. From your perspective, it is your hand that hurts. It is how we process an incident in our mind that amplifies the pain. Part of a reason we have consciousness at all is to direct our attention to injuries. It is a self-preservation method built into us. The concentration of thought is what is believed to provoke the healing agents in your body to respond to an injury. Your hand does not actually hurt, your mind tells you there is pain to heal it and create a memory for reference. The same is true with emotional pain. It is there to heal you and the wound is there to teach you.

Another aspect we need to acknowledge is the crossing of the threads. As our paths crisscross one another we will incur many incidents of pain and discomfort seemingly caused by others. We may think to ourselves, "I live righteously, I'm honest, I'm kind, I did nothing to deserve this." Unfortunately, this is the comedic drama of life. Don't be so grim. Do not despair. See the moment for what it is, an opportunity. Everything is opportunity if you know how to truly see. Maybe you can notice something about your attitude that needs to change, or your outlook on life, or on other people. Maybe this is the time to reconcile differences or chart a new course in life. Take this opportunity and be introspective. Look within at the deeper picture. Maybe you will find that your path has been laying the foundation for this incident to occur and you are not as much an innocent bystander as you would have liked to assume.

When we look around in our little world sometimes all there seems to be is brokenness. For some people this is truer than for others. Families have fallen apart, the community is in shambles, there's no economic stability, and trends like this can continue for generations. This life can seem very hard sometimes. We try, and we try but can never get a break. I mean it's like the whole world is rigged in some way. We might find that our hard work just doesn't pay off. No one appreciates what we do. Certainly, if there's a thing called luck then I just don't have it. What we really see when we are looking at things and perceive brokenness, in reality, it is *confusion*. Often this confusion is perpetuated by the environment in which we are born into. In this sense, it is in fact rigged so to speak. However, just because things are systematically depressed, suppressed, and oppressed doesn't mean there is no way out. We must learn to let go of persons, places, and things intelligently to develop and evolve. For these reasons specifically, we have the capacity for change.

Letting go of something is hard, but it is even more difficult to let go of when we are confused. You can imagine letting go of something that hurts you, that seems like a natural and obvious solution to the pain. What about the situations where we can't identify the source of pain, such as an environment, nutritional aspect, internal dilemma, or relationship? These areas and more are definite causes of pain, stress, confusion, brokenness, confinement, illness, and disease. From our world, to the nation, to the lower divisions of state, city, community, neighborhood, family, friends, and individually internally there is confusion and disarray. What makes it so hard is that it is all intertwined. We are caught up and affected by these existential circumstances whether we want to be or not. These are added stresses and burdens that we can learn to disassociate with through time and practice. For now, let's concentrate on some of the confusions that are closer to our hearts.

When we look at certain relationships, we cannot decipher why the word love is so intertwined with pain. It is a complex and confusing matter to say the least. As children, we learn by repetition, scolding, reprimand, and other forms of punishment including physical contact and abuses. In this sense, we learn to identify at an early age with love and pain. By the time we are young adults we have mostly developed a distorted perception of truth. By that I mean we have a limited perspective confined to what we have personally experienced. We may think that love hurts. This is not true. Love and pain are two different things, they are not inseparable, they can be isolated. You do not feel pain because you love someone deeply, it is not some hand in hand type of deal. Love and hate are the same feeling at different ends of the spectrum, as pain and pleasure are the same feeling, and happiness with sadness. This is where the confusion arises and causes us to cling to toxic relationships and detrimental patterns of behavior.

The problem lies in our level of understanding of true love, our misinterpretation of life's purpose, and our concept of reality. By nature, we are selfish, and that's ok. However, if you are looking to add others to your life as family or children there are things you need to know. To truly love is to appreciate something absolutely. To adore all aspects as seemingly perfect. There is no room for animosity, anger, or resentment where there is TRUE love. This level is only reached by whom we have considered saints or enlightened beings. What we have instead is a fear-based attachment to our expectations. What we want takes precedent over others. We lack confidence in ourselves to create our own happiness and opportunities. We learn to identify our results in life as complimentary to our compliments. We seek for in others what we feel we lack in ourselves. These defects in our character mold our behaviors and expectations of the world. Once we identify our shortcomings, we can learn to appreciate others. Until then we seek only to our own advancement. We have to learn. Learn to let go of our conditioning, learn to loosen our grips on expectation, and learn about ourselves. What do we really want out of life?

Perhaps the relationship was blissful, but was ended abruptly, leaving us broken and searching for answers. Undoubtedly this causes confusion. It can be painful to involve the time, emotions, and personal attributes of our lives with others. When it's all said and done it can feel like such a waste. Most of the pain we feel is misappropriated anger. We are mad that this person let us down. We are mad that they abandoned us. We are mad that for some odd reason we are always being left behind in one form or another. By adulthood we probably have a sense that life isn't fair deeply ingrained in our way of thinking. Maybe we even project this anger on ourselves. We might blame ourselves for them leaving, naming all sorts of reasons why we are no good. All this anger and pain too is just a misunderstanding, or belief that life's not fair.

They say that all is fair in love and war. I believe all is fair in life in general. All aspects, degrees, and values are included to encompass a balance and wholeness. We have to come to terms with balance and fairness as truth. Not only do we reap what we sow, but we also reap what is sown by others. Tied into the universality of cause and effect, our generations mold one and other. We are all in line for certain unavoidable consequences. This is not to be feared as it is a natural part of life. Do not fear nature. Yet, learn to cultivate positive outcomes through your intentions, thoughts, and deeds. At the very least learn to turn negatives into positives by way of your mentality but embrace them for what they are. Do not deny the pain, do not deny the hurt, feel it, and see it for what it truly is. Only a lesson, not a hindrance, but a catalyst for growth.

In the pursuit of happiness, we lose sight of our own value, or maybe never had a chance to develop it in the first place. The need to obtain a proper amount self-respect, and a definite sense of purpose is second to none in terms of personal value. If we know who we truly are, what we truly want, and where we want to go in life, being abandoned becomes less of a loss for you as it does for the one who left. I'll touch more on how to perceive and obtain personal value in following chapters. For now, I just want you to recognize that you only needed that individual or those people who played short roles in your life for personal growth. They arrived for nothing more than your personal development. So, thank them, for their departure was a lesson for you.

The most obvious pain we feel confused about is the seemingly random and untimely demise of a loved one. We all know it's coming, and we don't know when. Then it happens, and we are completely unprepared and caught off guard. We start to question it all. What is the meaning to all of this? Why do we have to experience loss? Why them and not me? Once again, our misunderstanding turns into anger and frustration. What we need to know about losing a loved one is that it happens. This life comes to an end. We take away lessons from them as they depart. What did they accomplish? What did they leave out? What did they miss? We take from our predecessors' invaluable lessons on time, energy, and opportunity. We can see in them things we value or dislike about ourselves. In their departure, it is not only their time for transformation, but it is also a time for us to reflect and adjust our course. It is a moment in which one is refined into a higher quality of being on the physical plane and the spiritual.

You may recoil at what I have to say, but here it is. Life is fair, life is brutal, life is hard, and when ours' ends life goes on. life isn't going to say sorry, when you don't understand it, life is not your friend. It doesn't stop and wait for you to catch up, life is also not going to hold your hand. When we have people in our lives who have said sorry, people who have waited for us to catch up, people who have held our hands, and ones who have comforted us through life's unforgiving training ground, we might define them as more important than life itself. In a way, we can identify with these individuals as the one genuine and meaningful aspect of life. It's hard to understand why they have to leave our sides especially if we believe they were put there by divine intervention in the first place. These circumstances can cause confusion and pain which resonates the remainder of one's life. The only alleviation provided is an understanding of the natural order. This understanding is usually a dismissive awareness of the harsh reality of death, but no true inquiry about life. Often the understanding we get is provided through our religious authority, family, friends, or perhaps in this day and age some information on the internet. Generally speaking it is not our own conclusions, but ones we received from others. In all these explanations you might miss this one absolutely imperative fact. The most important thing to take away from someone leaving your life is that *you have your own*. Their role in your life is no more significant than the role you must play in others'. Theirs has absolutely no more value than your own. Regard yourself highly.

Did this person play a significant role in your life? Did they at some point help you change for the better? Did they teach you that you can indeed overcome insurmountable pain? If you love this person value them today. There is no tomorrow, and there was no yesterday, all we have is now. Love them regardless of what they have done for what you have learned in the process about life. Take this moment to be thankful. Take this moment to make the changes you need. Take this moment for you.

Whether the answers to those questions is no or yes, those people were living their lives. So, you must live yours. It's hard to see our lives as individual and separate being so intimately involved with others since birth but think about it. No one sees life the way you see it. No one sees through your eyes. No one feels what you feel. Those other lives that have impacted us so greatly were on their own course, with their own experiences, their own expectations, seeing things through their own eyes. All that they gathered and felt about the world was for them. All that they did for you was personal to them. They have their path and you have yours. Sometimes in life our paths cross, but we all have our own story. Don't become so enchanted with someone else's life that you forget about your own. Your life, your appearance here, and your roles are divinely ordered. Never forget your own significance. Learn what you are meant to learn and continue your journey.

That seems like cold advice, especially in the face of death. When I think of broke, the most emotionally breaking aspect of life is death. It's also the most undeniable aspect. Up, down, rise, fall, life, and death are the immutable laws of polarity that we deal with. There's no sense in tiptoeing around the subject. We must recognize the pain of a loved one's departure for what it truly is. For us it's a cold hard blow to our own hopes and dreams. It's a punch to our own comfort. It's a knock to our expectations. It's a kick to the head of our complacency. For the person leaving it is a necessary transition. It is a stage of transformation. It is a revolution, it is an evolution, and it is a completion of a mission.

We generally wander through this life with no preparation for death. We ignore it as much as possible. It's scary and confusing to us that do not understand its necessity. Our trepidation prevents us from making a concerted effort in understanding this process. Most of what we might learn about death would come to us from one of two sources. One source about death being media platforms such as movies, news, music, social media, etc., brings us portrayals of harsh reality of life. The other being information from family, culture, and religious practices regarding eternity.

We get two perspectives on death in which we see very dramatic differences, both of which offer us little comfort in the scheme of things. One displays the gruesome and horrible effects that take place upon our biological organisms. The other riddles us the incomprehensible ideas of forever, damnation, and salvation. Neither of the two places do we learn about the true meaning of death. Why does one live and why does one die? Or better yet how do we properly prepare to face the inevitable, and when do we get the tutorial on how to live? When do we get to learn to celebrate this life and this thing called freedom? When do we get to learn what it's all about? Most will say those answers come when it's all said and done. I do not prescribe to this idea. What I have learned about life thus far has shown me otherwise. The answers are here and now.

I believe the true key in conquering the pain or sting of death, is in conquering living your life. We have to recognize death as a fact. It is transformation, no more, no less. It is undeniable change, the one and only truth. Everything changes. The purpose for it is in our development. In which we must prepare for it or meet it with uncertainty. We have to recognize the parts we play in each other's lives. We cannot just generally wander through and expect a significant outcome or legend to arise. We must learn to think, speak, and act meaningfully. We must be thoughtful of our surroundings, of our emotions, of our health, of our means, and of our ends. Think about the end of the day, the end of the week, the end of the month, and the year. Think about the end of your life. I'm not saying obsessively dwell on the end of your life but remain mindful. If life is accidental, then by all means accomplish little to nothing at all and wander about this plane. If life has purpose, then it is for you to decide how much to do, or in what direction to travel. The choice is yours either way.

Don't allow the fear of the unknown to paralyze you. Our interpretation of life and the meaning of death can either propel us forward or incapacitate us. I am writing this book to teach you that there is opportunity in every situation. Even the places we would least likely think to look. Poor little Timmy fell in a well and never came out. So, what arises from this situation? The answer is opportunities; for families in the village come together, for a local sign maker to create a sign that says, "Don't lean over the edge, you might fall in and never come out", for the workers at the cemetery to dig a hole, or it even could be a chance for a random dog to become a hero. Everything is a matter of perspective.

What do you want to accomplish? What do you want to leave behind? What can you change for the better? What roles are you here to play? Looking at the end is a healthy practice for living a fulfilling life? If mine ended tomorrow I would have gone in the midst of living on purpose. I have dreams of becoming an artist, author, and orator known throughout the world. I want to change people's perspectives on life and help them navigate the rough terrain. So, I must focus now and prepare for the unknown. I look to the future, and I look to the past, but I live in the present. I know that I cannot just relax today and work tomorrow. The specific results that I desire require me to be vigilant and adamantly pursue my goals. I create deadlines. I apply self-discipline which I have found to be highly constructive. Not waiting for instruction or demands from the outside world, I force myself into action. I have to type this right now because it has to be transferred to digital format from script. I gave myself 1 week, life happened, and it has taken 2 months to write this book. Now imagine if I had given myself a year or a lifetime. I cannot approach this leisurely for what I have learned. I must capitalize on this moment before it is gone.

With all the distractions, all the pain, all the fear, and insecurity in the world, it's easy to become complacent. Believe me when I tell you it has been immensely challenging to overcome my own sedentary lifestyle. Our culture breeds mediocrity. What I mean by that is, everyone settles. This is not an overstatement. Unless you are an enlightened saint you have settled in life. It's ok to settle for the things you want or need in life. What I have discovered is that many of the things that have become common practice in our lives, we do not want or need. They are monsters of habit. I'm not claiming to be perfect, I still settle in many areas. It's so much easier to robotically traverse this world on autopilot, but that ease has a tradeoff. Like everything else what is the opposite of comfort and ease? Pain and difficulty. Whether we reap that tradeoff now or in the future, the balance will occur.

PLEASURE

   Were all seeking it whether we admit it or not. Comfort and pleasure in every way possible. Either in this life or the next we want to attain bliss. We want it so bad that it is literally bottled and sold in every form imaginable. Think about it. Is there anything that is marketed, packaged, sold, that isn't catering to your attainment of pleasure? What can you offer others that will bring them joy and pleasure? What can you create? What can you do? What pleasurable things are hindering you progress? Is there such a thing as too much pleasure? Let's look at ways this desire for pleasure creates unlimited opportunities, and some of the aspects of pleasure that paralyze our potential.

   First, let's think about how we define pleasure. This is the definition as stated by Google;
pleas·ure

ˈpleZHər/

Noun

 a feeling of happy satisfaction and enjoyment.

adjective

used or intended for entertainment rather than business.

verb

give sexual enjoyment or satisfaction to.

Obviously, these definitions would be synonymous with happiness, joy, ecstasy, delight, contentment, and peace. We humans do a lot of things because they feel good. In the moment of indulgence, a rapture takes place and before we know it, we are swept into a world of which we have little to no control. Different chemicals alter the brain in many ways. Not only the chemicals we consume, but just as powerfully are the chemicals we produce naturally in the brain during emotional responses. These natural productions are good and wholesome. They cater to the development of our minds and bodies. They were designed to keep us safe and to facilitate our regeneration. If we're not careful our own system can turn against us. However, through thoughtful and educated conduct of the body and mind, we can be in control of the most powerful machine in the known universe.

The purpose for pleasure is obviously to serve as a guide. The opposite is pain, which also serves to guide us. The unfortunate part of this paradigm is the subtle ways in which the pleasurable things we consume afflict our minds and bodies with pain. Over time too much of a good thing becomes a bad thing. You might have heard the saying, "Too much is never enough". We don't have to take in substances like drugs or alcohol to be addicts, there are many forms of behavioral addiction. We see these addictions in everything common and unusual, from certain food, drinks, substances consumed, alcohol, narcotics, stimulants, depressants, video games, mobile devices, sexual gratification, pornography, shopping, etc. The list can go on to include all compulsive or consumptive habits. Not acknowledging this fact is a big area where society falls short in dealing with its behavioral/mental health issues. We don't confront these monsters because most of us live in a world that has stigmatized addiction instead of properly educating people about it. The emphasis currently is punishment of the dysfunctional. I am certain that most if not all people are addicts of one form or another. Probably not to the degree where you are incapacitated or losing everything over your issues, but somewhere within lies some troubling habit. The vast majority of people will never ever admit to, confront, or deal with these imprisoning aspects of character. Most don't know they exist and if they do see strong patterns or habits of behavior, they don't see the detrimental effects. Then there is the whole idea of how one would go about addressing these issues once realized. Therefore, they neglect to fix the problem until sometime down the road.

We are always seeking pleasure in this way or that way. With this in mind we can see that we have added things to the pleasure category in our lives that don't belong there. To understand how and why we do this I want to lightly delve into some sciences; psychology, neuroscience, and sociology, for a more comprehensive assessment. Let's begin with a dissection of the brain. Think of this as a little refresher course and try not to be too bored with the vocabulary and technical jargon.

SEEING TRUE PLEASURE

We have to go all the way back to biology class to start this little lesson. In order for us to navigate this plane of existence we have been equipped with organic supercomputers or brains for short. I know at some point in your life you heard of the pleasure center or the reward system. We are also familiar with the term fight or flight response. Well, when we are considering the experiences of pleasure and pain it all boils down to the level of survival. Is this situation dangerous? Does this food make me sick? Is it friend or foe? To complicate things even more we have our intellect, our interpretation of things, our beliefs. How do I *feel* about this? At the base of who we are we have these **hunger forces** that propel us forward through life. We have our biological animalistic drives, and our cosmic spiritual quests. We are a combination of physical and nonphysical. To deny one or the other would be a disservice to your arrival on this plane. Your internal longing for understanding and your natural drives for survival are housed in and operated by the same machine, both seeking fulfilment. Oh, the tangled web we weave.

The physiological response to environmental stimuli occurs as a composition of electrical pulses in the brain. Within this structure there is said to be more neurons than there are stars in the Milky Way Galaxy. Different areas conduct the necessary functions of life. Each part of the brain plays a specific instrument so to speak. Visual functions, motor functions, emotions, linguistics, memory, etc., are all hardwired together in a crisscrossed compression of neurons. Some of these are automatic and we have very little direct affect if any on their function; heartbeat, respiration, digestion, and growth to name a few. Others, we have the capacity to manipulate; movement, observation, communication, etc. All functions and systems of the brain and body are directly affected by how we conduct ourselves in totality. What we eat, drink, hear, see, touch, taste, sense, think, speak, and experience, we embody. They say you are what you eat, but in this reality, you are the composition of everything you experience. That being said, we can see how important it must be to guard ourselves from what we consume in every sense of the word.

Think of the transmission of experiences in the brain basically like an interstate mix master between major cities. The traffic being neurotransmitters such as; dopamine, serotonin, endorphins, adrenaline, norepinephrine, etc. (These carry specific signals). The neurons are the cities and towns from which the traffic flows (sends messengers from experience or to experience). The interstate is the axons or paths between neurons. The areas of the brain are like states (pleasure, memory, sight, sound, attention to detail). Generally, in life the brain follows a stimulus to response type of pattern. Green light means go, yellow light to slow, and red light stop. The signals control the traffic. Over time and depending on the neurotransmitters involved, the brain can develop an imbalance, deterioration of the infrastructure, mixed signals, and dysfunction if not properly maintained. Repetition of experience either physically or mentally causes new construction, which is meant to reroute traffic, or accommodate the influx of population.

Starting with what we eat, drink, or taste it will be easy for most to see the impact this has on your mind and life. Obviously, we have to eat, and drink to survive. Well at least this is the most common consensus across the board. There are references of individuals, gurus, or enlightened people who are said to only get their vital nutrition from the sun and have no need to consume food or drink. For the rest of us 99.999 percent of individuals, we neeeds our fooods! My kryptonite is chocolate; brownies, cookies, cakes, and pies. Not the most nutritious, but surely the most delicious. Sorry if I just triggered anyone, but that was kind of the point. Within the complexity of the brain's communication there is little space for intention. Once we consume something in any way, the signals begin firing off and automatic processes ensue. You don't have to taste or smell something for automatic responses to begin. Even the simple thought of something will create real physical changes inside you. The mind/body machine usually takes control. They say that we only consciously direct our choices 5% of the time. The other 95% of our lives are being directed by subconscious programming. We easily get lost in routine.

In a healthy mind and body, the traffic flows smoothly. If there is an interruption the brain counterbalances accordingly. Too much traffic is rerouted, slow vehicles to one side, litter and contamination dissolved. We see, smell, or remember food and begin the mission to fulfill that specific desire. We reach for the food, consume it, and document our experience. Our pleasure center in the Limbic system takes note of its surroundings and remembers the environmental circumstances for future occasions. Patterns and habits form in the brain like a beaten path through tall grass or snow. Once the foundation for a specific path is formed the brain prefers to repeat that direction. Eventually a formidable path is constructed. If the habit is not healthy, happy homes along a path can be demolished in the name of eminent domain. Most frequently conscious interjection is bypassed. This can be where those sweets turn sour.

We consume! More than eating and drinking, we consume. We breathe the air around us and, in that action, those microscopic particles enter our blood stream and become little pieces of our physical structure. What we hear and see we epitomize. Next time your standing in a group or speaking with friends take note. Your posture, their posture, type and tones of voice, gestures, we all mirror our surroundings subconsciously. When we see images on a screen or in life, let's say a traumatic event, for instance the World Trade Center's burning. We internalized that moment. All the content that surrounded that event becomes ingrained in a part of our belief system. Our thoughts, actions, and reactions to the environment regarding high rise buildings, air planes, and people of middle east descent will be forever ingrained in our subconscious. (*side note I am conscious of propaganda and mind programming and therefore do not subscribe to the mainstream consensus surrounding these events.*) The information about an event changes you even if you are not directly involved. Being informed makes you involved. Informed- *to give shape to, form the mind.*

The formation of these connections in the brain can be likened to the beaten path I referred to above. The more times a certain activity is repeated, the more solid and easy the connection occurs. Regarding consumption this is where pleasure and fulfilment can become misconstrued. We start out in life as blank slates. Now just think about every time you tasted a certain food such as sugar. Can you even fathom how solid the paths surrounding the sugar experience are in your brain? Definitely established hard routes in mine. Now take that simple idea and apply it to any experience in your life and you will see, if you look carefully, how imbedded specific behaviors can be. There is a distinction to be found between pleasure and fulfilment. Pleasure is the temporary gratification, the hunger impulse was fed. Fulfilment is the attainment of natural balance and harmony. One is a temporary fix; the other is a long-term goal.

There are elements of this earth we are naturally meant to consume to keep us in balance, garner health, and maintain homeostasis. Without going off the deep end so to speak, there are many things out there were not *supposed* to consume but are *allowed* to. In fact, major industries commit crimes against humanity in the name of making a profit. The companies may be innocent in their intentions, seeking gratification as a body with needs and wants. However, they say ignorance of the law is not an excuse. In this age of information, it is impossible for a destructive organization to not recognize the implications of their actions. They are perhaps not as consciously developed or ignore facts to sustain their reality. The wheels of the machine are turning, and the momentum may have been propelling it for a hundred years. Such and antiquated organization is usually so fixed in its patterns and methods that it must continue until it extinguishes its resources or consumers. At the rate of progression in this technological time we will see the demise of many of the polluting industries. By polluting I mean they contribute to the destruction and not to the construction of a healthy society. I also recognize that the destruction is a necessary element of construction. The field must be tilled to plant seeds. Until society patches these wounds for the benefit of future generations, we must work to identify the pollutants among ourselves. We have to be informed and take matters into our own hands for goodness sake.

This section isn't meant to be a rip on pleasure, it is to create a distinction between the necessary and excessive elements of it. So, let's look out into our society a bit and view the human experience from an anatomical and anthropological perspective. We all have these innate drives as I mentioned before. We are searching and learning constantly. Our attractions and repulsions pull us to strengthen bonds and mold our personal preferences. We also have these especially unique skill sets, talents, and features that add variety, depth, and interest to our lives. We even have some passions and drives that go beyond what we have learned that stem from our essence. These are the things that makes us question the universe, question our roles, question our family, society, culture, and ourselves. They drive us forward and backward. Sometimes we get stuck in a cycle and go around and around.

The most amazing part about this is reflected in nature. In the changing of the seasons, a new blanket of snow, a wind storm sweeping sand over our footprints, the fresh spring foliage beginning to fill an old path. The brain has what is referred to as neuroplasticity. It grows and forms new paths with new information, patterns, and habits. What we learn is not fixed. We can continually grow and transform. If we are well equipped with the conscious direction of our thoughts, words, and deeds, these barren fields we see will soon become fields of plenty.

So, what's broke in your life? Is it really broken after all? Or is it a catalyst for change? Is this moment an opportunity incognito? There are no wrong answers. There are no wrong choices. There are no accidents. You are where you are by design. External and internal influences have created your reality. All that surrounds you is tied to you directly. What you eat literally becomes you, what you breathe becomes you, what you think becomes you. When you know this, you cannot think that you have no influence on the outcome. Clearly you do. Where you place yourself, who you surround yourself with, what you consume. All that is broken is because you view it as broken. If you do not want to be a part of this broken environment then change your surroundings, change your thinking, inform yourself, conduct life differently. If you have tried but feel you cannot succeed hang tight and read on.

CHAPTER 2

A CHIP AND A CHAIR

Miracles, coincidence, and synchronicity

The term miracle brings about a variety of emotional responses; from skepticism, to hope, to happiness, awe, and disbelief. For some people the mention of the word miracle will throw them back in time when an unlikely event occurred in their life. Maybe the mention of miracles will take another person to the extreme opposite end of the spectrum and incite anger. In both cases, we will find one common thread. The expectations of these individuals had been shattered. These people's concept of what could happen in life were shifted. The one who gets angry, resentful, or defensive about the possibility of a miracle had tried to believe at a young age. I assume they prayed, or wished upon a star one too many times, only to have their dreams go unanswered. Now they have built a wall out of their dashed hopes. My intention is to get to a reasonable understanding of miracles in this chapter. In the end, you will find that it is the readers interpretations of the words that determines their understanding. Also, in life, our *interpretation is key*.

I'm certain all of us have had instances that happened when we were in the right place at the right time. I'm sure all of us have uttered the exact same words as another at precisely the same moment. Everyone has had the experience of déjà vu where they felt convinced the exact scene in life had already played out. Most people will agree that there is an important invisible aspect to life. Those same people will call these coincidences random events. Coincidences and synchronistic events are funny little hiccups in life's orchestra that make us momentarily stop and question the order of the universe. We cannot help, but be awe struck by the timing or sheer magnificence of certain worldly things. They are a brief glimpse into the connectedness. Again, viewing these incidents as ordinary, magical, or otherwise is a personal endeavor. I propose that one seeks to understand or view these occasions openly and not to dismiss them.

We see that there is an underlying order to this word in the animal kingdom, the planets, and all of nature. There are hidden laws which dictate all. We look at human beings as separate in a sense. Most people see us as in this world, but not of it. The composition of a human is the same as other animals, but the mechanics are exponentially advantageous to us. So, the underlying thought through much of the world especially the west is that we are here above the animal kingdom. We are here with the capacity to dominate and therefore should.

What does our connection and dominance over animals have to do with miracles? Simply put it is in our collective perspective. In this world, it seems that the theme is "Eat or get eaten". We lose sight of the hidden connections that binds us all. We ignore the facts that we are all in this together, that we arrived in the same fashion, and that we are essentially the same. I'm not implying that you are just an animal, we are an advanced species. However, denying our worldly ties and commonalities is to deny yourself in a sense. There is a deeper well in which we all drink from. It has been said that we are all one body. To deny this inference could be considered delusional with all the present evidence. Simply look around you at all the fluid movement of bodies. Take a look at the flow of traffic or the sound of a busy crowd and you will see. The seemingly chaotic and individual is in fact an organization, collectively a song.

In order to capitalize on an opportunity, we must recognize one when we see it. Exposing corresponding events, and miracles for what they are will lead us to a closer connection to our truest nature and purpose. To get there we have to come to a basic understanding of the fundamentals of our connectedness. Nothing can be proven as fact beyond a reasonable doubt. We must consider the evidence we have been given through our senses and trust them to be close to accurate. At least for the purpose of navigating this world, our senses are all we have to rely on. When you understand that this fact is what makes anything true, you have a key most people never find. My reflection in a mirror is not what I look like to other people, that is why we are often uncomfortable with our own image in pictures. The reflection is a reverse image, flipped horizontally. The picture is the direction others see from. Perspective and understanding determines what truth is individually.

Throughout the millennia people have been gathering empirical data and conjuring up theories to discern the meaning of life. All the great scientists, theologians, and philosophers the world has produced have developed our modern concept of reality. To summarize this as basically as possible is to say that the physical world we live in is not exactly physical. When you break something down; whether it be a human, a tree, or the seat you are sitting on, the basic fundamentals become elements of energy. What everything is or becomes springs forth from a pool of potential for anything and everything. Once you can see that all the building blocks of life emanate in the same form, from the same source, then you will realize the correlation between your thoughts and reality. Everything is opportunity. The most basic element of anything in life has lying dormant within profound opportunity. The chance to become something, the chance to do something, have something, give something, all is not chance, but is opportunity. You have the opportunity to become something, the opportunity to do anything, the opportunity to have, or give whatever you will.

So, what is a miracle? What is a coincidence? To me they are no more abstract or mystical than everyday life. Life is a miracle in itself. Why are we so blown away by the idea of a miracle inside of a miracle? A coincidence is simply two sides of the same coin, they belong together, they are one. It is a front and back at the same time. A coincidence exposes something entirely as it is. These are both very comprehensible concepts once observed through the proper lens.

If you are anything like I was most of my life you dismiss miracles with a, "Yeah right". I was always too busy looking for a pot of gold at the end of the rainbow to stop and marvel at the rainbow. Who needs a pot of gold when you can be fulfilled by the sight of a rainbow itself? At this point that might sound cheesy. However, after you take a step back and look at the entire process, a simple rainbow becomes mind boggling. I was too busy looking for an obvious sign, a direct quote, that said, "This is God speaking". In my search, I failed to recognize the significance of the dirt beneath my feet. Why bother with the who, what, when, where, why of the creation? Being filled with gratitude and awe by the experience of life itself puts you on an entirely different playing field.

I look at miracles, coincidences, and other synchronistic events as guidelines in life. They are part of the underlying pattern over which the fabric is laid. If we're allowed the opportunity to witness such occurrences, I believe we are receiving a gentle nudge in the proper direction. Being aware of these moments as they arrive is paramount not only to the preservation of life, but to the fulfillment thereof. This guidance is an inner knowing that we all have. It is suppressed in most cases but can never be extinguished. Being aware and observant as the guide lines appear is one thing but preparing for them to appear is another. What I propose is that we can not only prepare for miracles but create them. It is our level of conscious awareness that determines to what degree this transpires.

In the recovery movement, they say, "Don't give up before the miracle happens". In the employment field, it's, "Suit up and show up". 6 or 7 years ago, I taught myself how to play Texas Hold'em no limit poker. I thought I was really good at the game after practicing it for several months. I used to challenge my family and friends to a fun little game and taught most of them how to play it. I even believed I was good enough to win the world series of poker. I was inspired by the plays of these professional strategists I watched on TV. I was captivated by the risk they would take pushing all their chips in on a bet that they had the best hand. This was especially true when they were putting it all on the line with a stone-cold bluff. In the poker world, there's a saying too, that all you need to win is, "A chip and a chair".

Jack Straus was an American poker player about whom the saying had originated. As the story goes Jack was down to one chip in the main event tournament at the world series of poker. He ended up coming back from that undesirable position to win the entire tournament. If you know anything about the game, you can relate to the challenges he was facing with one chip left. With increasing blind costs, a field of the world's best competitors, and the devastating blow to morale with one chip, he was miles away from being a prospective winner. Also, take into consideration what was on the line. This tournament today costs about 10,000 dollars just to enter it, and the grand prize is somewhere in the tens of millions. Talk about heart palpitations.

As the story goes, Jack should have lost the tournament ending up on the rail as one of the many spectators. At some point in the first day or two of the tournament he pushed his chips, "All in". This move turns out one of two ways; really great, or really bad. Well he lost that hand and was wiped out of chips. As he was about to leave, he looked down to notice that he had one chip left. All he had left at this point was a chip and a chair, but maybe he had more. Jack went on with that miraculous chip to win the World Series of Poker that year.

A miracle would have been just winning the tournament in the first place. Not to mention that a lonely chip would alter his future to have him jotted down in the history books. This is what I'm talking about when preparation meets a miracle. Jack was a professional. He was known as one of the best bluffers in the game. He dedicated his time, energy, and resources into developing his craft. He homed in on his skills and capitalized on this opportunity. The cards in his hand didn't have to be the best for him to win. He took what he had and made the best out of it.

Was he in the right place at the right time? Definitely! However, he was there with the intention to win. His hard work and skill got him there, and his creativity and determination got him through it. The cards were stacked against him and the chips were down, but he took that devastating blow and transformed it into opportunity.

In such a defeated position, it's easy to give up. When the odds are daunting our minds begin to play tricks on us. We start to think things like, "Better luck next time" or, "It just isn't meant to be". This is where the cultivation of a positive mental attitude will determine success or failure.

There's no doubt Jack had a challenge ahead of him, but he was prepared when the miracle arrived. A chip, and a chair, and so much more. Maybe there was no miracle, or maybe he was the miracle himself. Maybe he needed to hit the bottom to see there was nowhere to go, but up. Maybe

Jack's story isn't so different than our own. When we get to our lowest point we can give up and throw the last chip in on a whim, or prepare, change our perspective mentally, and hold on. We can wait for the opportunity to strike, or we can create the opportunity we need out of that chip on our shoulders.

You might be thinking at this point, "That's an inspiring story and all, but winning a poker game isn't how I quantify a miracle." I'm willing to bet old Jack would say otherwise. He probably considered that chip a God send. What we view individually as miraculous doesn't agree across the board with all people. For instance, just because I have never seen a ghost or apparition does not disqualify these occurrences from existence. In my life, a ghost doesn't hold up as real. My concept would deem it as a holographic imprint of an event in the fabric of space time. However, I am also very aware that reality is determined by the observer. So, to someone else they would see a haunting image. I remain open to anything as possible. My hope for humanity is that we reach a point in our civilization that we don't all seek adamantly to disregard other's experiences. Rather, we embrace and quantify each other's experience as real and meaningful. I believe this is the direction of the people inevitably. We are all one in this quest. The outcast among us are an essential part of the cast. What magnificent contributions lay dormant in the mind of the destitute? Unseen miracles. It is that which is within us all. Potential, and possibility are the words that describe the building blocks of this universe. Opportunity is when the observer, YOU, meet that potential. The chip is your potential, the chair is your chance, and the game is your life. What will you make of it?

The primary reason for our disbelief in anything including the miraculous is from our heavy cultural conditioning. If I cannot see it, then it must not exist. In our society, we're taught to question everything, just don't formulate your own ideas of truth. Many who would be considered non-conformists fall into a category labeled with some nasty connotations; atheist, conspiracy theorist, anarchist, etc. When we hear these terms, we automatically associate them with the mold our media, education, and political authorities have outlined. Though, the rebels, the rejects, the crazies, the lost souls of this world are the ones who move us forward. Most world changing ideas were not initially accepted. Their thoughts and actions created revolutions. They are those who see what most cannot. The question is what are they tapping into?

SEEING MIRACLES

Just take our sight for example as it is one of our primary senses. How can I doubt its authenticity? To be blunt, I cannot. I also do not draw conclusions based simply on my sight alone. After all we don't see what is truly there in the first place. Our minds conveniently package these images in easy to assimilate versions of truth. Our brains can only process so much information at a time. It has to take bits and pieces of the whole and seam them together in your mind for a fluid scene. In this process our eyes do what they can, and our brains try their best. However, they leave out so much detail they cannot be exclusively trusted or relied upon entirely. Hence, the other senses.

My beliefs are not concluded by my sight. I understand the hidden aspects of life make up as much as is out in the open. Some people are more perceptive naturally, and others have worked to open themselves to higher levels of awareness. Some have stronger bodies, stronger minds, or other aspects about themselves that set them apart. Some have stronger senses which also include those which are not commonly recognized or referred to. They can include different modes and levels of intuition, instinct, extrasensory perception, clairvoyance, and other psychic phenomenon.

Without diving too far off topic I want to include this very real aspect of human life. As I mentioned in the beginning of this chapter, we are all connected through an unseen field. It wirelessly tethers all things. Maybe I can illustrate this field for you. Take a second while you are reading and blow on your hand. What did you feel? Your first thought will be wind obviously, but what is wind or air really? You just moved an invisible substance, a pool of elements and particles. This invisible something caused you to physically feel something touch your skin. We are so accustomed to the wind that we never think more than a second about it. It's just part of our nature, our environment, like water. That vast expanse of seemingly nothingness surrounds us, encompasses us, and connects us at all times. The "nothing" that is outside us pervades us.

If that observation alone is not mind blowing miraculous then I'm afraid not much can be at this juncture. The point of this chapter is to take us out of our conditioned way of thinking. We are in what I will call the old paradigm of the miraculous. In the old way of perception, a miracle is a weeping statue, an angel formation in the clouds, stigmata, or raining frogs. Once I began to see regular day to day events for how truly astonishing, they really are, my appreciation and understanding of life grew exponentially. Another focus of the chapter will be on patience, perseverance, and optimism. It's my goal to help the reader see how our conditioning molds our level of production, our lucky breaks, and incapacitates us at times.

Have you ever noticed that the most popular inventions seem to be no brainers? I can't even count the amount of times I heard or said to myself, "I should have thought of that." It's the simplest things in life that are most commonly overlooked. The things we all take for granted. The regular, the mundane, habitual, or routines in life just become part of the norm and tend to lose their luster. More often than not the simplest solution will solve the most complicated problem. Usually we are our own problem, we are the complication, and we too are the only solution.

The hardest things to see are the things we do day in and day out. The way we talk, the way we carry ourselves, the food we eat, who we associate with. These are the things that make us who we are. Through some careful observation of the ordinary we can unlock our greatest potential. Perhaps you're the type of person who always journals about their day. What you might find is your life's calling has been begging you from this simple task from the beginning. You didn't know that you were inclined to inspire the world with your thoughts and ideas until a loved one comes across your journal and implores you to feed the world with your words. Maybe that same journalist never sees their own hidden talent and after they pass on their words live for time immemorial through a relative's publication. Finding our calling requires that we observe the levels and stages of our life. We must objectively view our direction, past, present, beliefs, values, traditions, and dreams.

Things change fast in our modern times. We feel like if we don't keep up, we will be left behind. This urgency makes us want what we want, right now! The sooner, the better. It seems like we're all in a hurry and going nowhere fast. People speed around you just to end up beside you at the same red light. Like Ricky Bobby once said, "If you ain't first, you're last!" Somehow this became the normal way of life for most of us. I recall the words to an old song, *"I'm in a hurry to get things done oh I rush and rush until life's no fun, all I really got to do is live and die, but I'm in a hurry and don't know why."* A little patience goes a long way. Have you ever been just frantically trying to accomplish some tedious task? The more you hurry, the more you fumble, and the more things go wrong. You were already in a hurry and now this is just slowing you down more with each mistake. Then you calm yourself down, slow down, focus, and concentrate on the task and within seconds you succeed.

I'm all for acknowledging life is short. If you're going to do something, there's no better time than right now to do it. I believe we must act, and do things we want, or feel that we need. This action however should be aligned with your true purpose, a natural calling, and concur with your highest principles.

For many years through my late teens and early twenties I hardly had any real values to speak of. I loved my family and thought I was a good friend, but my actions didn't line up with my ideas of myself. At that time, I was conforming heavily to popular culture and had no real sense of purpose, direction, or goals. My motivations were self-fueling. I did anything I did out of creating my own sense of security in this world. The fact is I was scared. The same is true for my personal relationships. I may have authentically cared for someone, but my actions didn't align. Uncertainty about the future I wanted for myself caused me to never truly commit to one path. I took being in a relationship as a form of security in my youthful ignorance. I didn't recognize the other human had dreams, goals, wants, and needs to be fulfilled. Nor did I care. I wanted to hang out, laugh, and piss my time away in bliss, in lust, in companionship. Around and around we go. Deep down I knew I was going nowhere fast, with the girls I knew I had nothing *real* to offer. I gobbled up that denial routine. I clung to ideas like I am young, I never had any guidance, I thought I had that *bad boy* routine and really knew no other way. I, a boy, was teaching myself how to become a man.

The time was starting to fly by. A lot of it was being wasted. I would work a 9-5 that was comfortable, easy perhaps. There was no challenge and not much of a future. I always excelled wherever I was but ended up holding myself back for it was never the future I truly wanted. I would work just to get a paycheck, just to spend it on drugs and alcohol to forget my problems, just to end up creating more problems that I needed to forget. It was a vicious cycle. It was like I was just living a life, wasting my time, waiting for a miracle. I hoped and prayed something magical would just come and change all my circumstances for the better. Gambling and playing the lottery were part of that weekly routine. I felt like I needed divine intervention so that I could become happy and whole. It never dawned on me at the time that my whole experience was in fact divine. I was stuck in limbo waiting on my old perception of a miracle.

The problem being that I was never taught, as most of us, to effectively cultivate the future of my dreams. What I ended up with is a lot of cleanup work to do. I had to organize the shambles of many separate paths. I had to teach myself how to set goals in life, in business, in family, in friends. I had to teach myself new ways to live, healthier food choices, healthier emotional choices, and healthier information consumption. I had to change my environment inside and outside of myself.

I realized the only reason life was speeding by is because I was ignoring it. I was afraid of the outcome because I didn't know how to create the ends that I desired. I ended up a long way down a road I didn't want to be on. I knew it was headed for destruction. Either physically or emotionally I was going to end up distraught. I needed out. I kept looking for a hole in the fence to escape, but it always looped back around. I finally realized I would have to forge my own path intentionally.

The people that surround me probably think it's a miracle how much I have changed. All I've really done is began to see life itself as a miracle and align my actions to reflect my gratitude thereof. I could no longer take life for granted. I knew there was a better life waiting for me, I just had to find it. The changes began with an inner certainty that I could do better. I recognized some coincidences for what they truly were, divine guidance. As with anything it takes practice. You begin to notice the subtle nuances, what I call the hidden guides, and instead of brushing them off, embrace them.

We are all a work in progress. We must work for progress with an honest conscience if we are to succeed at anything worthwhile.

WHAT A COINCIDENCE

You wake up in the morning and for some reason you have the chorus to the most annoying song stuck on repeat in your head. No matter what you do trying not to think it or speak it, the words just keep going, over and over. Not the best way to get out of bed in the morning, especially if the words you're uttering in your mind carry a negative message. You think to yourself, "Why on earth am I singing this song, I hate it in the first place?" You continue about your morning routine, which I am almost certain never deviates. Off you go, hop in the car and boom there it is on the radio, that wretched tune. Did you predict the future? Or were you somehow tapping into the present? If so, was it the mind, the body, both, or neither that played a role in this wireless tap? What a coincidence, right?

First, how about we ponder what a coincidence is? The word itself as defined by google;

co·in·ci·dence

kō'insədəns/

noun

noun: **coincidence**; plural noun: **coincidences**; noun: **co-incidence**; plural noun: **co-incidences**

1.

   a remarkable concurrence of events or circumstances without apparent causal connection.

2.

correspondence in nature or in time of occurrence.

3.

   PHYSICS

   the presence of ionizing particles or other objects in two or more detectors simultaneously, or of two or more signals simultaneously in a circuit.

What do we find in the definitions? Well, the words origin comes from coincide which means "go together" or two of the same. We see that it is events that go together in nature, (as in the type of situation) or the timing of the situation. We also see that there appears to be no causal connection, as if these two things happening are independent from one another. While these definitions give a good explanation of what a coincidence is, they don't do it justice in terms of how a coincidence happens. The definition in terms of physics helps us to dive a little deeper into the word. We see in this definition the presence of ionizing particles or *other objects* in two or more *detectors* simultaneously. Consider if you will the radio, and your mind, or body as the detector/receiver. The "other objects" as the FM signal. At first you might not think your body can receive radio waves, but it picks up sound waves, light waves, and absorbs every other non-visible form of energy around us. It's not a stretch to consider our capacity to assimilate data through invisible wave forms.

What I find most intriguing about this topic is the idea of suggestibility. This is how coincidence is related to opportunity. How much influence can external signals have on our lives? Or, how much influence can one have on nature through the production of their own mental waves. Are we susceptible to certain programming? Do we have the capacity to alter the physical with the mental? I for one am convinced all of this and more is at the very core of our reality. We can easily be dissuaded from believing we have any real effect on the nature of things. What happens to me was going to happen regardless of how much mental energy I put towards avoiding it. This may be true on the grand scale of things. If the asteroid is coming it's going to hit no matter how much I tell it not to in my mind. However, what if the asteroid's appearance is only an effect of the collective collusion of thought energy? Perhaps all the promulgation of fear plays the most critical role in the actual appearance of horror.

As I am writing about in another book <u>Modern Chains,</u> the creation of and access to such advanced cellular technology comes with it quite a few unseen costs. Nowhere in the fine print will we see the warnings regarding the mind altering affects this technology will have on our lives. The scientific evidence supports both sides of the spectrum and is inconclusive whether these wireless devices contribute positively to our mental and physical health or negatively. I postulate the idea that the unrefined mind and body will be highly susceptible to negative alterations from this technology. I am speaking about what we see and hear through these devices as well as what I believe can be transmitted directly into the body and mind via radio wave and electromagnetic frequency. Even if you don't want to dive off the deep end of conspiracy, you cannot ignore the mass consumption of visual and audio stimulation this generation is *receiving*. All of what is absorbed will play a critical role in the mental development of individuals in proportion to the exposure thereof. This fact cannot be denied. So, is it coincidence that we see and hear things on our devices after we think about them, or is it programming? That may be a thought for later investigation.

So how does a coincidence happen, and what are the implications? We are transmitters and receivers. You can chop up your explanation of the song playing as the first definition of coincidence, a random accident of similarity, or you can see the connection and role you play as integral. The choice is yours and there's no wrong way to eat this cookie. I suggest that we are more than bystanders, but actors, instigators, and provocateurs. Our thoughts and actions have a broadcasting affect. The more tuned our mental faculty is, the deeper our level of perception will be. Our level of physical and mental health correlates to the level of affect we have on our environment. I speak more on the *refining* process in later chapters. For now, I just want to touch on the capacity to send and receive information via the mind and body.

We can see that a coincidence is better understood as process of correlated events. The harder part to see is our influence on the circumstances. The song is being broadcast, and my mind happened to be in tune. Picking up radio signals is not the important take away from this section. What I want the reader to gather is the awareness that the body and mind are more than just processes. We don't just think, live, and maintain homeostasis. We actively mold our surroundings with our presence alone. Couple this with our capacity for imagination, creation, and other outward expressions, and we have a recipe for unlimited potential. Learning to cultivate an open mind, develop clear thoughts, limit incapacitating behaviors, attitudes, and concentrating on purposeful efforts will open the corridors of meaningful and beneficial coincidences. These synchronistic events will help guide you to your correct path. Being receptive to them allows you to garner a greater appreciation for, and understanding of, the meanings for your life.

DEJA VU

I'm not exactly sure if the feeling of déjà vu is experienced universally by all people or if it appears only among a select lot. I don't know if it only happens among certain cultures or groups. I don't know what variables make you more susceptible although my interpretation of it suggests that it happens more the younger you are. This phenomenon is a little spookier and less likely to be understood. As with most things in life, the observer will develop their own personal interpretation. This is my perspective on the topic as it relates to opportunity.

You might have experienced this sensation before. You enter a room or pass by certain buildings and you get this flash of insight. It is like a shift, or split, or repetition in the fabric of time itself. All the sudden it dawns on you that this exact moment you are experiencing has happened to you already. It is as if you're living in another dimension simultaneously. How did this happen? You know for certain you have already lived this excerpt of time. The people around you enjoy your brief delusion as you scramble to tell them all about it. "You were there, and you were there", pointing to the witnesses in the crowd. Almost as if it happened in a dream. Was it a dream? I suppose questions like this will remain shrouded in mystery.

I believe alternate dimensions and levels of life exist, as do most of the people alive, and in recorded history. All cultures talk about the world after this one, or the world above this one, heaven, hell, etc. This may be hard to fathom at first, but I will do my best to explain what I mean. What is a dimension in terms of reality? To me a dimension is more than a shape. It is a perspective, an understanding, awareness, knowing, and being. It is not only a type or aspect of an object, that description is the very lowest level on this plane of existence. It is all encompassing. It is expansive. No barriers exist in the dimensions of reality except the ones we impose upon ourselves. A dimension is used to define the parameters of an object, but this can only be done in three dimensions. Our perception beyond 3 dimensions in this life is limited.

Imagine you are walking through the desert. All of the sudden a wall appears before you. It is painted white. Now the floor is gone, you are floating, and the wall is all you can see in every direction, the wall you are viewing has 1 dimension, flat. Now you look to the right and you see a line, the corner of the wall. Your eyes follow it up and you see the top. Now you are perceiving the wall with two dimensions a width and a height. You make your way over to the corner and realize there is another wall just on the other side that continues forward. Now you have a length, a width, and a height, and you are perceiving what you thought at first was a flat surface as a cube, 3 dimensions. The next dimension is the Immeasurable perception of the observer itself. This observer sees in shades of light, shadows, and perceives in time. In the 4th dimension you have transparency. The cube becomes clear, you can see it from every angle, and move in and out of it. Now picture yourself floating away from the cube which is transparent and permeable. It's getting smaller and smaller. All of the sudden your back bursts through a clear membrane of some sort. As you continue floating away you see that this was the barrier of another cube which is now shrinking as you float away from it. This is the best I can do to illustrate what dimensions are.

We have the capacity to penetrate certain dimensions in this reality. 3 with our bodies and 4 with our mind. To me the observer is the 4th dimension and the observer of the observer having the capacity to manipulate would be the 5th.

Now let's get back to the topic at hand. To illustrate déjà vu, I want you to picture the process of the life of a tree. The tree is your life. As the tree begins its journey there is one path, the trunk of the tree, long and straight. At the first major life altering event the trunk splits into two. Now this split can be caused by innumerable things from moving locations, to deaths in the family, to any number of circumstances. At this first split the life continues down one of two paths. However, the other path which was not followed continues forward in an alternative dimension. As more life choices and situations deviate our course, we continue to branch off in different directions. My perspective of déjà vu describes this phenomenon as our alternate dimensions of life coming in contact with one another. So, this is where the branches of the tree of life so to speak cross each other. When they cross it is déjà vu which is there to guide you on your journey. This occurrence lets you know that you are on the right path.

That no matter what decision you made in the past, all the alternative choices would have led you to the exact point you are at currently.

Moving forward from this point I hope you have a little clearer picture of those mysterious events. Not only do we get to witness these miracles and coincidences, but we play active roles in their happening. The most pertinent aspect to recognize of these instances is the guiding roles they play. If you are open and aware when they occur, you will see your path more clearly, make better decisions, and be able to capitalize on potential opportunities which otherwise may have been overlooked. Be open. Cultivate a little optimism, some patience, and perseverance. Miracles happen, but they are no more miraculous than everyday moments. So, revel in the glory of everyday miracles. Let the coincidences and déjà vu remind you of the role you play in your own life and that of others. Be mindful that the orchestra doesn't sound the same without your instrument's harmony.

CHAPTER 3

WILL WORK FOR CHANGE

Life will do for you what is necessary for change to occur. Whether you intentionally direct your path or haphazardly go with the flow, you are affecting change. We create our outcomes whether we know it or not. Most of us don't recognize the power and influence we have over our own life. We like to be in control. We want to be in control. However, this power is only coveted when things are going the right way you see? When we end up in a situation we didn't want we blame life for being brutal and unforgiving. When things happen how we want we tend to be a little more egocentric, "I'm the man" so to speak. Figuring out how much influence we have on the outcomes of our life can be challenging. Sometimes we see things as fate, and other times we see cause and effect. Let's unravel the mystery of change.

We are all progressing from one end of this journey to the other. How and what we develop along the way is personal and necessary for our individual evolution, and for the totality of mankind's progression. Our talents vary, looks, voices, fingerprints, etc. All of these variations will continue to unfold until every possible outcome has been exhausted, indefinitely. The reason for the variety is that life expresses itself in every way possible. The micro resembles the macro. This should be inspiring to know. It is up to you to determine whatever specific outcome you choose. How do I know that your path is not predetermined? Conclusively I cannot boast with unattainable information. All I can give is reason and rational evidence to support my hypothesis. A dandelion is a dandelion, but it is still a unique expression of the Plantae kingdom. Out of all possible plant life expressions it is the little yellow flowering root we know so well. It has its own special properties that make it what it is. A person is just a person, but what can or will be done by an individual is unique, special, and necessary. Furthermore, you are an expression of life, on this plane of existence it is easy to see we have alternative choices. Within the confines of specific natural laws, we can do whatever we will.

When our paths crisscross one another, we gain certain life experiences which influence the different outcomes. We meet certain people and go through what we do to become the highest version of ourselves as possible. Like a purification process so to speak, we become a filter of other's characteristics. Although, oddly enough the only purification that needs to take place in our lives is of those things we have absorbed from others. A catch 22 type of thing. A lot of us will never do the work necessary to refine our characteristics. We pick up our habits of speech, interaction, ideas, and everything else from others and rarely shed the bad traits. We enter life pure and gather contaminants along the way. Very few will spend their life in the purification process or fasting in the desert. Most don't even know they've been contaminated. This too is perfectly fine. Everyone will become who they will. As I said before ALL expressions must be fulfilled. Therefore, no matter what you choose to do with your life, your choice is perfectly correct. It can be no other way.

I personally believe there's more to life than just being a variation of it. I find there to be subtle higher callings which require a cleansing of the mind and body. Specifically, I feel that the human life on earth experience is a spiritual training ground. Ultimately enlightenment is the graduate stage. This is where I stand on this topic currently and am ever learning and adapting my perspective.

For necessary cleansing to occur there is self-awareness. How aware we are depends upon what extent we are willing to go in pursuit of our truths. One thing I know for certain is that you are on the right path already. Even if you feel lost at times or can't figure out your purpose. You and the universal intelligence are co-creating your highest version of self. The only drawback is we have the option to ignore this calling. Being born into this life set you in your own little channel. As the river flows down throughout the land it may break off from the source and carve a new way in the land, but it always comes back to its source. When it dries up and evaporates it is reunited with the whole river again in the atmosphere. The creek may have gone down a narrow path alone, but it is always connected to where it originated.

Our lives can be likened to this river. Whatever path you choose is perfectly fine. You will find that the farther you stretch from the source the harder it will be to keep your momentum. Your channel is your own life. Sticking with the path you carve or finding your way back to origination is the only natural direction you can take. Inevitably there will be many rocks and hills which divide us and hinder our growth. Evidence of what water does to a rock in the way can be found in grand canyons around the world. Persevere and you will find your way. We may also find our channel meeting the path of another river and gaining exponential momentum. The babbling brook and the raging river all have their purpose, to facilitate life. The creek that finds a way around all obstacles after being separated may create an oasis from which new life can emerge. A personal aspiration of mine is to become an oasis if you will, a well, spring, launching pad for the disenfranchised.

The point I'm trying to make is that you are what you are. You can be what you will. Nothing about you is wrong. Nothing you choose to be or do will be wrong. Life goes through evolutionary cycles. Some choices in life lead us down harder paths then others, but we all get to where we are going one way or another. The purpose is to facilitate life in whatever manner you choose. This may be only the preservation of your own life, if that is what you are called to do at this juncture.

Some people feel like part of their life is missing. Maybe they sense a higher calling. As if they have a duty which they have not fulfilled. This emptiness causes people in their ignorance to clamor for vices, environments, and people to distract them. Filling the void in any way. If you so choose to elevate your consciousness, rise above the influence of contamination, and evolve your being entirely, then you must take certain steps in that direction. You have to get in touch with yourself, develop a relationship with the divine aspect within; identify problematic thoughts, feelings, and situations, positively support your life, and create an environment which caters to peace and harmony.

Cleansing the Mind, Body, and Soul

So, let's say I've run a bit off course. Along the way, I picked up a lot of pollution. As I went throughout the land, I absorbed toxins from this place and that. I was filled with other people's trash that I carried along. Do I want to carry all this back to contaminate the source? Do I want to continue this direction? If I meet another river, I would surely pollute it as well, if I have not been through a cleansing process.

I want to give you a glimpse of some short term and long-term recovery processes. Applying techniques like this in my life allowed me to get back to homeostasis. Creating a more natural and balanced life for myself I was then able to find my callings and seize otherwise unseen opportunities. These introspective processes require applying information or resources to gain a more wholesome understanding of self. Questions like who am I, what am I doing, what do I want, and is this the right path, can become very cloudy. Trying to find answers to these questions in murky water is almost impossible. For this reason, specifically, I have created this part of the book. To see how everything is opportunity, we must first identify why we cannot see the opportunity yet. Then we have to do what it takes to get a clearer perspective. Finally put to work some habit-forming methodology that keeps us on track to our highest purpose.

Getting to a level of harmony and balance is not easy. It takes effort, there will be battles, and you will get knocked off your square. However, the more in tune you are, the more you live in the zone of harmony, the easier it gets. After a while you will find that not much bothers you. You will sense the truth immediately when you see it and hear it. The best part about getting in touch with yourself is clear personal insight. Noticing when you're putting yourself at risk of any negative consequence.

Processes for re-alignment

People all around the world rely on different methods for learning, concentration, peace of mind, health, and wellness. Though our techniques for centering ourselves vary, the goal is alignment. Life has a natural balance and harmony. Our busy lives can throw us out of whack. The more distractions the harder it is to stay aligned. Pretty soon we find ourselves years down the road on the wrong course. Most of us are putting things in our bodies which have alienated us from our origin of wholeness.

In our modern culture we will find many elements which are toxic to the mind, body, and soul. Indulging in these things are part of the life process. However, many of these elements have the potential to hijack our direction, deceive our perception, and sever our connections. Continuous exposure to these toxins will create diseases of the mind and body. The hardest part about identifying those elements is the fact that many of them are socially acceptable and culturally welcomed. Trying to distinguish between safe measures and harmful amounts of certain things can be a very arduous task. Most of the information about things that are harmful is backed up with scientific support from special interest groups. So, in your inquiry you will find evidence to support the benefits of a thing and evidence to the contrary. It is up to you after thoroughly investigating these elements to determine what is right, and good, and natural for your life.

Here is an unconventional list of things that I have determined we should personally investigate.

- **Associations-** Who do we spend our time around? This may seem odd for the list of toxins, but it is at the top for a reason. We become generally an average of our associates in terms of ideals and lifestyle. Finding those that are conducive to your highest vision for yourself will advance you considerably.
- **Entertainment-** This is also very important for your overall health and wellbeing. The sounds, words, and images that we absorb have a direct effect both consciously and subconsciously on our actions and beliefs. Overexposure to negative connotations, and explicit, or violent imagery formulates your perception of the world in potentially harmful or detaching manners.
- **Consumption-** You are what you eat, but not only that. What you drink, what you breathe, what you ingest from any orifice of your body is adopted by your physicality. We are comprised of elements and can be destructed by elements. Not only do substances alter your mentality and physiology, but sights, sounds, and other sensations that are stimulated can as well. This area can be especially challenging to learn what is right and good for you.

- **Employment**- We spend 1/3 of our life sleeping, 1/3 of it in leisure, and 1/3 of it at work. At the age I am now 34 the estimate is that I have slept for 11 years. Considering the fact that I have been working to some extent since before I was 14, including school, it only makes sense to examine this area of life.

After your thorough investigation of what is good for you and what is not, then you must take steps to re-align. The cleansing process deals heavily on information and action. What we learn we must apply in order to get back to as close as possible to our starting point, before we contaminated ourselves. Here I have made a list of 10 forms of meditation that will help regain harmony in life. These can help counter balance some of the more arduous parts of life. Things like; Reading, Exercise, Meditation, Prayer, Athletics, Hobbies, Diet, Travel, Education, and Vacation. While undergoing these activities our brains get to enter a "flow state" or level of frequency that is euphoric in a sense. This peace of mind and concentration enables healing modalities and invigorates our sense of being.

All these things and more can reduce stress while strengthening natural drives. They help bring balance to a fast-paced world. When we get overwhelmed or distracted by the world, these things can bring us back to center. From this point we can properly see direction and hear natural guidance.

THE 5 KEYS FOR A HARMONIC LIFE

(IM IAM)

1. *INTUITION*

: The ability to understand something immediately

Some people say the starting point for change is desire. Either we reach a point where we can no longer continue in one direction, so we must change course, or something dramatic happens and alters our course for us. I believe the starting point is intuition. Unfortunately, intuition is so easy to overlook. This aspect of life usually gets a, "Hmm, that's interesting" and we go right back to business as usual. We've all seen the subtle guides. The things in life that remind us of what we wanted, what we are called to do, insightful glimpses into the future of our current course, even random "miracles" begin the alignment process. These insights are what create the desire or motive in the first place. For instance, me wanting to quit smoking cigarettes was not why I quit. I had insight. I could see what was in store for my life if I continued that path. I could also remember what it was like before I started. I had an inner calling speaking to me that said, "This is not your highest purpose". That vision of what was to come if I continued smoking did not line up with the path, I knew it was most natural for my life. Those insights, that gut feeling, and intuition is what created the desire to change my habits. That intuition came from the source of my being.

There is a place of natural balance and tranquility that resides deep within us all. The subtle guiding forces never leave us. They may become harder to see and hear the further we get away, but they never abandon us entirely. It is up to us to listen to them and know what to do when they arise. Once I heard the intuition, I had the motive to pursue my goals. The first key is hearing the intuition.

The intuitive process is natural and always occurring. However, we become cut off and detached in the hustle and bustle of our daily lives. Tapping into our natural intuition requires harmony, but also creates harmony. We must conduct our days in a certain manner in order to use this bountiful wellspring. Hear no evil, see no evil, speak no evil, do no evil. This little quote may sound like a no brainer, but it's easier said than done. Of course, we don't see ourselves as evil beings. I am not speaking of the evils such as terror, war, and crime. I am not talking about villains and criminals. If you're at that level of evil, this book probably isn't in front of you now. I am talking about what we do to ourselves and others daily. The things that trap us in conformity, facilitate disease, hatred, jealousy, and self-destruction.

In life it is easy to gravitate towards certain actions that cater to what we view as rewards but are in actuality vices. As I spoke about in the section on pleasure and pain we can be distracted from our natural callings by dwelling on and living in *emotional trances*. The reward system built in our survival response area of the brain can get distorted and misaligned through traumatic events, personal/social exchanges, and chemical manipulations. Understanding how these events may have altered our behavior as adults, gives us the ability to heal and restore our mental health. We should be introspective and educated in the how and why of our actions. Even if we don't understand the process entirely, just being aware that certain choices may be occurring automatically can clear up our intuitive mind.

Intuition, being one of the keys to a harmonic life, will be understood best from a cultivated perspective. The level of awareness and insight we have can be elevated through concentrated effort. Eradicating the subtle evils, and subduing contaminating thoughts, promotes health, happiness, comfort, ease, and prosperity. Other ways to tap into intuition include prayer, silence, meditation, and seclusion in nature. Intuition happens in a flash. We get the sense immediately upon our actions or thoughts. Whether something is good, positive, and natural, or mischievous, harmful, and distasteful we sense it instinctually. We know if something is harmful or beneficial to ourselves and others. In the pursuit of the ego and other potentially detrimental aspects of self-centeredness we may put this awareness of evil doing to the side and take what we feel is a small gain for ourselves. In the grand scheme of things these events probably don't matter much, but over time we may be developing self-gratifying habits that not only hurt others but hinder our own growth and potential permanently.

The insight never leaves us. Always begging from some hidden avenue of the mind. Once we recognize the vital role of this aspect of our minds, we should protect it, and nourish it. In In order to do so we will eat natural food, drink clean water, breathe clean air, and stay active in our lifestyles. By bringing our physical bodies into a natural balance we strengthen the flow of electrical currents, nutrients, and chemicals throughout the body. Optimizing the bodies healthy output and input we forge a channel in the unseen field which unifies us with the universal body. This creates reciprocity between what we see, hear, do, and know, to what we feel, sense, and believe. Ending in a clearer channel of intuition.

2. *MOTIVATION*

: The reason or reasons one has for acting or behaving in a particular way

This is probably the most important part in the entire process. This is the ingredients, the bread and butter. We can look at motivation in two ways. Both of which are very important. You might hear things like motivation is garbage, motivation gets you no where, etc. The people that dismiss this key are missing a huge component to the achievement machine and opportunity capitalization. One thing you might not associate with motivation is that it can be both positive and negative in how it propels your life and actions.

Let's start with negative motivation to end on a good note with this subject. How can motivation be negative? Read the definition one more time. *The reason or reasons one has for acting or behaving in a particular way.* Ah yes, now it may have sunk in. The reasons I act or behave may not have been consciously directed with sound mind and body. Perhaps I spoke or acted out of repetitive programming. Maybe my motivation for doing something was not on the level of where I know my actions should be.

So, there are forces that drive us. What we believe, or how we act are influenced by our past. Knowing this we will use our intuition to help us settle the dispute of whether or not our motivations are in alignment with our highest purpose. Clearing up the negative motivations we can then move on to the best aspect of motivation, it being a driving force which can make us unstoppable.

The key is motivation and the notes comprising this key are purpose, love, and acquisition. You could say that motivation derives its power from these 3 notes. Freud would say that your motivation boils down to two things; sex and aggression. Eros and Thanatos. Life and death. Either you are pursuing the creation and preservation of life, or you are attempting to overcome your adversaries in any way including aggression to protect your territory. We are seeking purpose, love, and acquisition unconsciously in as many ways as we can to secure our species, bloodline, genetics, and heritage. When we can see this consciously, we can more effectively direct and control our negative and positive motivations.

Being motivated is a fundamental aspect of this life so participating in the just motivations is being in alignment. Following the motivated path and exercising clear judgment will yield fields of opportunity.

3. *INFORMATION*

: *Facts provided or learned about something or someone.*

Once we receive the intuition, and are motivated properly, we must begin thinking critically about our path. The most important aspect of thinking is having the capacity to critique our concrete beliefs and ideas. Obtaining a better understanding of our conditions and choices we make should come first in our pursuit for info. First, we seek to better understand ourselves, our bodies, our machine, our mental faculties. Without informing ourselves of our being we cannot then decipher our truth from cultural pressure, family pressure, manipulative propaganda, marketing, etc. How will I know who I am and what I truly want and need if I never critique my own beliefs. Secondly, we inform ourselves on the vast array on information available that caters towards our specific true callings.

As we enter this arena keep an open mind. Remind yourself that you naturally have bias towards specific answers and genres. Become adaptive and malleable. If you meet resistance within yourself to identify with a topic, take note, the universe is speaking on a learning moment. Try to focus on information that builds the mind, body, soul, and character. Don't let the distracting disinformation consume your energy. Keep your focus on yourself. Fill yourself so that your cup may runneth over. Gather new knowledge from as many sources as you can. Read, watch videos, listen to speakers, meet professionals, surround yourself with people who also inquire about the good life. The more you can learn the better you can be at whatever it is you want or desire. With all information available in the palm of your hand there are no excuses to not use this well of opportunity every single day to better yourself.

Taking what we thought we knew and coupling it with what we continue to learn creates a unique expression of our potential at the highest level. Everything is changing, there is no constant in this dimension of experience except change. Apply this to everything you think you know, and the windows become clearer. Recognize in your learning and adoption that truth is subjective. We will all apply emphasis to that which we personally deem truth. Whether consciously or unconsciously we naturally form what we are learning to fit in the box of what we want the truth to be. This is perfectly ok and natural, so long as we recognize why we feel a certain way about the subject. Be informed so that you may create form.

4. *ACTION*

: The process or state of acting or of being active

All the keys in fact are elements of the action that needs to be done. Technically it must happen from the moment of intuition. However, I wanted to include action near the end of this section because it will be the planning and preparation that gets us where we need to be in order begin implementation (the real problem solving, the outward demonstration of our inner truths). Or, maybe I'm just a procrastinator and so my actions always come last after contemplation. Either way action is an obvious component to this harmony. There are different types of action which we should be cognizant of. There is physical and mental action, and in both types of action it is the habitual in which we find the tangible results in our lives.

So, in order to get our actions in alignment with the natural harmony we must follow the keys in order. First intuit, you get that gut feeling. Keep in mind your gut has brain cells just the same as the one in your head. You have two brains and one is in your gut, hence the term, "Listen to your gut." Second, we must use our motivation. Use the whys of it all to propel us daily towards that which we value. Third key is to inform ourselves about ourselves and our motives as much as possible. 4th key is to act.

Action and follow through is the ultimate step in realization or creation. We have done the planning. We have learned what is necessary to continue down the right path, now we put the pieces together and solve the puzzle. Our highest life calling can seem either so far away or it can fall right in our laps. Once we see what it is, we must work. We must continue this process of learning, development, and action if we are ever to have an affect on the world or realize our true callings. If you don't yet know what your life calling is, continue to read and the answer will become clear. For the time being we might have to become actors and not directors. As my dad use to tell me, "Fake it until you make it." Move confidently, but not arrogantly in the direction of your dreams. This will align you with the natural harmony we may have lost adapting to this strange and busy world.

We are all actors in a sense developing our characters for whatever role we need to portray in life. We have many roles which are important to note, but more importantly are the masks. As an actor in the drama of life I am a father, son, brother, neighbor, employee, artist, writer, and many other roles. Actually, I only have about 4 masks. I have the Shane my family knows, I have the Shane my associates see, the Shane I view myself to be, and the Shane God created. I have a feeling one of the, if not THE mission(s) in life on earth, is to merge the 4 into the true 1 self. As we create these masks and fill these roles, we learn to adopt feelings, attitudes, and habits. A lot of these can be negative developments. Attitudes of pessimism, habits of poor thought, and language, detrimental consumptions of all types transmute our progress. If we do not acknowledge them as a façade of harmonious life and act towards cure, these can and will become hardwired. Too long down any road will create permanent effects. We will identify as particular masks that are not authentic to who we are or were made to become.

Day in and day out we are performing tasks. Many of which we do not even need to do. Many of which hurt us and hinder our progress. Action is imperative to our success if it is in the right direction. Awareness of our habits is a must. Most of the habits I adopted unwittingly were not of benefit to my life and were contributing factors to my self destruction. I am still in many phases of weeding out what I view as character defects. It can be an arduous process. All the positive habits I have formed have been through conscious information, direction, and application. Now would be a good time to take a break from reading and do some writing. Let's take note of some habits we have developed by way of society, family, and cultural programming. Also, a list of habits which we have made conscious directions in our lives.

Unconscious	Conscious
• assuming the worst	Drinking lots of water
• eating what tastes good	Smiling more
• Cursing	Thinking positive
• Promiscuity	Reading
• alcohol, tobacco, drugs	Healthy hobbies

Following these keys, we reach the final note which ties it all together. The last letter in the acronym and final key for establishing a harmonic life is maintenance. I struggled with choosing between maintenance and mastery for the final key. I chose maintenance because without it there will be no mastery in life. Also, this section is devoted to developing harmony and balance, not striving to achieve anything extraordinary.

5. *MAINTENANCE*

: The process of maintaining or preserving someone or something, or the state of being maintained.

We all get little bursts of inspiration and motivation from time to time. The fizz in our pop goes flat after a while if the desire is not maintained. If we don't keep a high level of healthy habits and conscious motivation our ambitions will be swept under the rug of complacency. To keep our attention, we usually must see results. We should see that we are progressing in an elevated direction. What better way to see results than to continue to establish a comprehensive understanding of our best interests?

To maintain the harmony, we have created in our lives we might have to take some major steps. At this point in the process we may come to a cross road with some pivotal decisions. Maybe we have to cut ties with certain individuals which we have come to recognize as more of a liability to our success than an asset. Perhaps we look ourselves in the eye once and for all and ultimately drop a part of ourselves we held onto for so long. We could finally seek professional help to deal with a situation which we have neglected to confront. Many parts of the maintenance process will be a lifelong battle. Just because we have formed new habits and paths for our minds and bodies to follow doesn't mean that our programmed machines don't glitch. The automation that went on for so long wants to fight you for the easiest way. Your body and mind will try to deceive you for a long time. It will try to trick you back into your old way of thinking and acting. We should hold our ground as much as we can. Fight the temptations. Fight the out of balance impulses. Maintenance of peak mental state and body balance does get easier. Persevere.

Maintenance won't be as much forced as it was in the beginning to find motivation and stay motivated. We will at this point have many more resources at our disposal. From new companions, new hobbies, new perspectives, and new ways to live our lives, we can pick from a plethora of positive distractions. When the doubt creeps in it can't stay for long in the new environment. Fear, loneliness, illness, and even disease will be met with a new level of mental and physical fortitude. Health in every sense of the word becomes the new norm.

IAM was created to be an in-depth reflection on the self. Everyday and in every situation, we find ourselves saying I'm this, or I am that. When we pronounce that I AM this or I AM that we are creating a declaration for the universal field to help us mold. When we think, we begin the process of manifestation. When we think and speak, we are forming subconscious routes for behavior. When we act, we are binding with external demonstrations. Using I am forms belief of expectations. I am is not to be used indiscriminately.

If I say I am trying, then it implies there is room for failure. This statement will lend the user the luxury and leisure of not trying in the future. In the event one fails after trying they have a get off the hook free card of saying, "At least I tried. If I say I will then it creates a level of accountability. Now I have to find a way. Not only have I formed this challenge to my ego, or my higher self, but I have declared it aloud for anyone spectating my performance.

I have concentrated the 5 keys for a harmonic life in a manageable formula, with an easy to remember acronym (IM IAM: Intuition, Motivation, Information, Action, Maintenance). I chose this acronym specifically because of the reference to the name of God in the Old Testament. When Moses met with God and was called to retrieve the Israelites from Egypt, he asked God, "What shall I call you?" To which God replied, "I AM that I AM." I find it peculiar how this was the response and thousands of years later we use this exact phrase in English when declaring something about ourselves. When I realized this, I became cognizant that I should use reservation or caution with what follows I am. Not to declare I am weak, or I am sick, or I am tired, or follow it with a curse word. For there is hidden power in language and thought, this I have come to recognize.

Within the 5 keys are the workings of the machine. On the surface you see 5, but within each are the elements for consciously creating your future.

In order to get where we want to be, we have to see things accurately. We must know where we have been. We have to make adjustments in our course wherever necessary. These changes are not easy to say the least. Depending on your age and how long these previous habits and conditions have had a grip on your life, determines the challenge you face in changing them. However, don't let the size of your problem deter you from creating a solution. You can overcome the set backs, you can overcome the fear, you can overcome any obstacles between you and your goals. How do I know? I've never been in your shoes. Well, for one I am not trying on your shoes. For two, we are equal. For three people have overcome greater obstacles than you or I combined. Here are a few stories which may put your position into a more agreeable perspective.

Against All Odds

Everyone fails in life, but what can be seen by one as a failure, to another is success. Some people's failures are on a plane that is higher than most people's goals.

Names like Stephen King, Samuel Jackson, Stan Lee, Henry Ford, J.K. Rowling, Oprah, need no introduction. They are known around the world for their works. They have become some of the most successful people in their industries. Like everyone, they have suffered major setbacks, losses and problems in life. Many of the people we recognize as icons today were no more different than you or I were growing up. We like to think that people of notable positions have received some favor or luck in life. It was simply preparation and persistence. We use the excuse that they were favored to justify our incapacity to perform at a high level. Really, we each have the capacity. Some things come naturally, and some things can be taught, but we can all succeed.

Perhaps you've heard of K.F.C.? No? O.K. well let me enlighten you. One of the largest resuraunt chains in the world is adorned with an iconic picture of a jolly old man. No, not Santa Clause. I'm talking about Colonel Sanders. Harland Sanders was 65 years old when he created K.F.C. By the time one reaches 65 we think of them as generally winding things down. Mr. Sanders had marginal jobs throughout life but believed in his fine recipe for chicken. He knew he had something special. When his lifetime of preparation met his commitment to see his dream come true, there was no stopping the ensuing success. He was prepared, he had a plan, and carried it out. You can now see Harland Sanders (Colonel Sanders) face on over 18,000 K.F.C. outlets around the world. He never gave up on his dream. He made changes to his plans and adapted to the market. He took the knowledge he had and turned it into an opportunity.

The name Samuel Moore Walton probably means nothing to you. However, the name Wal-Mart is undeniably engrained. Whether you shop there or not, you know what it is. Walton was a business man who owned and managed several grocery stores, but he had a different vision and didn't see eye to eye with his business partners. He wanted to provide a discount retail store to the more isolated and rural areas. At 44 years old Sam Walton created Wal-Mart. When I wrote this, it was the worlds #1 grossing company, with annual sales close to 500 billion dollars. This could be considered an unlikely prospect for a rural farm boy, but in the course of Sam's life he had an intuition which he never let die. His preparation met that intuition with open arms and catapulted him into unprecedented achievement.

The future is unknown for everyone. It's a level playing field. We can either fear this uncertainty or plan and create. We like to think that we are planning and creating our future by getting a good paying job with retirement benefits. That's all fine and well as I mentioned before, any choice is perfect and natural. Although if you have a dream, if you have an intuition, if you have a gut feeling, don't let that die. We all have a special, unique, and specific purpose. Once it makes itself clear to you, I implore you to find a way for it to be done. Having your inner calling come to fruition will give your life a feeling of wholeness and purpose that no ordinary job can fulfill.

If the future is uncertain already then why would you let the uncertainty of pursuing your dreams stop you? For me the biggest fears about my goals try to stop me all the time. The challenges never go away they just transform. We will always have an obstacle of one form or another. The objective is to equip yourself with the tools to handle them. Live will make you learn how to cope with things, or you can teach yourself how to deal before the problem occurs. Part of my mission in life is to share my experiences and the knowledge I have gained in dealing with them. The possibility of my writing helping someone forge through their challenges adds purpose and peace to my life.

Without being of service or creating I get an unsettling feeling. Although I know it is perfectly ok to just be still and experience life as it happens, I have an itch to affect the process. I have a calling to creatively address the world. Through my writing, my art, and inventive ideas, my purpose expresses itself. At this point if I were to give up on my dreams for the safety and security of a weekly paycheck and 401k retirement, I could still find a way to be content and happy. I understand that my attitude in life is not determined by my circumstances, but how I can deal with the things as they happen.

Work is work. Action is necessary. No matter if I do what I love, or love what I do, do I must. Opportunity is everywhere. This is not some hip hip hooray cheer. Literally everything is opportunity. A chance to make something happen. The pen that I am holding has immeasurable potential. Depending on who picks it up, and when, changes everything. The fact that I happened to pick it up today wrote this page. Who knows who will read this page and be transformed? Who knows the outcome of this decision? I know what I intend for it to be, but who am I? Just a guy from small town Iowa.

I want to end this section with one final story to close out this chapter. Its about a girl who overcame tremendous adversity. Her faith and determination prevailed to make her an unlikely success story.

She started out in life as a poor girl from New Orleans, Louisiana. Her father was a fisherman and her mother tended the house and educated her to the best of her ability. They didn't have very many books and she didn't receive any formal education. Times were tough back then.

Mother introduced the young girl to a pastor from a local parish. Pastor John was in his seventies by the time he met the young girl. He began teaching her about the bible, and how to read, and write. A year had passed by the time Pastor John noticed the bruises on the young girl. He didn't question right away, but eventually was compelled to ask where they came from. She was reluctant to tell the old man because she loved her Pa. After all she was defying his orders to stay home while he was at sea.

She ended up telling Pastor John about her troubles and he contacted the local authorities. Later that night when police apprehended the girl's father, they found a note on him. It was a suicide note in which he apologized to his wife and daughter for harming them all those years.

After her father left, her mother fell ill and passed away. At 13 she was orphaned and sent to live with relatives in Chicago Illinois. During her stay with her aunt and uncle she faced even more hardship. Her aunt and uncle abused alcohol and prescription medication. This turned out to be the turning point in her life. The abuse she endured from them caused the state to relocate her once again. This time she was placed in an adoptive family.

From here she took her adversity and transformed it into something beautiful. The girl went on to higher education graduating from the University of Virginia with a doctorate in Psychiatry. She went on to establish the Marianne Williams School for Orphans. In 1962 she was awarded the Nobel Peace Prize.

The reason I added this story is to demonstrate how our perception will influence our reality. What we think is real is as real as what is real. It doesn't matter that the last story was entirely fictional. You were already inspired by the previous stories of hardship and adversity. You know from your own experiences that life can be challenging and yet you have the potential to overcome anything. I just wanted to drive home the idea that even the most miraculous stories are actually normal. They are within our reach. No matter the challenge, it has been done, or will be done. The question is, when you create your future, are you planning for the miraculous? Will your story be one that is written about some day? When you bump into an old friend will you capitalize on this coincidence in life or will you assign it as insignificant?

My intention for the reader is to strengthen your awareness. By the end of this book I hope to help you see the guiding order within the chaos. Things that are normally overlooked are incidents which you have attracted to your life by way of thought and action. We all make our own beds. At first glance this can be very hard to see and understand. With practice in observation techniques, self awareness, and mental control we can become masters of our destiny.

Use the 5 keys to a harmonic life as a basic guide to understanding peace in life. They will help you find center, build momentum, and accomplish meaningful direction. These keys are as basic or as complex as you want them to be. They are designed specifically to cater to the broad and vast experiences we each have as individuals. Though experience varies greatly, the path in which we create meaningful and purposeful ends are the same.

CHAPTER 4

GOD

Belief is intrinsic. There really is no way around it. It is a part of who we are. Written in our code, stamped on our souls, woven into our beating hearts, we are no more than we believe. Few facts of life are inescapable and our need to believe is one of them. As we come closer to understanding how everything is opportunity, its necessary to take a long hard look at what we believe.

To believe in something or have faith in it is to trust in the unknown. We all believe in numerous things throughout the day. Although, our belief in these subtle circumstances are generally unconscious. Time has taught us that we need not constantly fear things. When we sleep there is trust and belief that we will awaken healthy the next morning. When we venture out during the day, we have faith in our modes of transportation that the mechanisms will not fail us. When we sit down for dinner with our families we pass around the food and indulge in it without fear. We have faith and believe the food is wholesome and good for us.

Every single action we take can be attributed to belief in one way or another. We naturally and perhaps highly unconsciously have developed our belief systems. It is part of our nature. This idea goes back to our intuition, our essential being, the fabric of creation. Over time we begin to see how the world works, and how things are tied together. Our experiences in this life give us incredible evidence to trust and believe in certain things. We don't need to see each and every stair to walk faithfully up or down the staircase. Though, I have watched my older sister trip going up the stairs several times in life. Maybe she didn't truly believe in the stairs or something, I don't know. Falling down I understand, falling up, not so much. I digress.

Belief is a powerful thing, quite possibly the most powerful tool of the human mental capacity. I know some would like to place knowledge or reason at the highpoint. Knowledge to me is just the highest degree of belief. Nothing is certain, as soon as we think a thing is this or that certainly, new evidence comes along and changes our perception. Knowledge is just the perception of corroborating evidence appearing to be true. Any challenging evidence to that knowledge dismantles the certainty. Therefore, the most someone can have is a strong sense of belief that something is true or false.

WHAT YOU FEEL YOU THINK YOU KNOW

The degree of feeling, thought, and belief you have of something determines its relevance to your life. What you feel you think you know about something can be quantified to determine the level of significance it has in your life. If you want to know how much something is affecting your path just put it to the test. This is simply a fun little evaluation I developed for this book to help you connect with your truest self. For instance, if you want to know the importance my job has to me, I would use the word "JOB" in the evaluation. Only assign one bubble to each question or phrase; Either you feel (x), you think (x), or you know (x). The narrower and more specific your subject the better the results will be. If none, mark unknown.

To feel something, it will be like a hunch or an urge maybe calling from inside nothing more. To think means you have given much thought to this subject, but not much practical application there is still a high level of uncertainty. To know means you have investigated this inside and out, this is a belief in life based on experience. Unknown means either this does not apply, or you believe the answer is false.

F T K U

1. This __ has the power to control the entire outcome
   of my life.   ( )( )( )( )
2. I cannot live without ____.   ( )( )( )( )
3. I'm thoroughly informed about____.   ( )( )( )( )
4. This _____ is a part of me.   ( )( )( )( )
5. I can change_____.   ( )( )( )( )
6. I want ____.   ( )( )( )( )
7. _____ should be a part of my day.   ( )( )( )( )
8. My purpose in life involves____.   ( )( )( )( )
9. I can give up _____.   ( )( )( )( )
10. I need ___.   ( )( )( )( )
11. I created ___.   ( )( )( )( )
12. I give ____ for the good of humanity.   ( )( )( )( )
13. I am not emotionally attached to___.   ( )( )( )( )
14. I dislike ____.   ( )( )( )( )
15. _____ Is healthy.   ( )( )( )( )

After we have completed the evaluation of a subject, we will assign a number for each column. Unknown = 0, feel = 1, think = 2, know = 3.

0-10 = This score would indicate a few possibilities. First of all, if you have not had much contact with this subject maybe you should work on strengthening these connections considering you were interested enough to plug it into the exam. If you have had contact with the subject for years and it takes up much of your time, maybe you should look into leaving this behind and exploring something new. A score of 0-10 shows me that you are either overthinking the exam or you are trying to separate yourself from the subject intentionally marking unknown. Either way I believe it is time to explore a new path or subject.

11-20 = Anywhere on the scale from 11 and up indicates a strong mental, physical, or emotional connection with this subject. You have spent many hours cultivating this relationship. Now just because you feel, think, or know something to a high degree does not mean it should consume your time. Yes, these subjects are important to your life and have made a strong clear impression but may not be in your best interest. Perhaps what should be investigated the most are things with the highest scores, from 20 to 30.

I hope you enjoyed the exercise. As I mentioned this was just to help you look at things from a different view. Applying tough questions to things we normally never question can be an enlightening process. I encourage you to write down or think about the things that are a part of your everyday life. Think about what they mean for you as an individual on this life long quest. Some things are meant to play a small roll and we cling to them incessantly. Other things are meant to play a larger role and perhaps we continue to overlook or push these things to the back burner. I think you will find that the things that are meant to be there for the long haul will continue to re-occur in your life without your conscious direction. Hints from the guiding field will pop them into your life spontaneously until you take hold of it and direct it purposefully.

MIS-UNDERSTANDING

What we feel we think we know is just a segue into what we don't understand. The things that keep us down or keep us stuck like prisoners in life are the things we don't understand. Either a thing is veiled in complex or obscure terminology, or we might not have access to a subject that is out of reach, maybe the dissemination of information on a subject has been manipulated, or it could be that a thing is in fact not knowable through empirical evidence and research.

Some things in life require a blind belief and that can be scary for several reasons. One may be scared to believe out of the fear of looking ignorant to peers. Everyone wants to be in know, so to speak. We all want to have comprehensive understanding of topics, tasks, or subjects which give us an advantage in some way. It is a primal instinct to dominate in whatever manner possible. Another reason one may choose to adopt a belief without inquiry is the pressure of society and conformity. This can be disastrous and or profound. As they say, "Ignorance is bliss". The adoption of a belief can cause unparalleled shifts in events. Good or bad is irrelevant, the power of belief is the subject in question. To avoid looking ignorant we have 3 options; 1 deny the belief altogether, 2 blindly accept a thing as a cultural norm and ignoring alternatives, 3rd is to gather information and knowledge developing a personal belief and relationship with the topic.

It is the misunderstanding which binds us to pain, to confusion, anger, and insecurity. We have indirectly and directly been misled in life. Which, in turn causes us to intentionally or accidentally misguide others. It's a vicious cycle that we easily get swept into. No matter what field or area of life we look, beliefs abound. Where there is belief there is misunderstanding lurking in the shadows. From language, learning, life roles, family, food, culture, religion, etc., we have all blindly accepted things in life as they have been presented without further inquiry. This is a dangerous game especially in this fast-paced day and age. Where it used to take a millennia and ages to alter the course of history, now it can change within moments. We have always been connected, but now we know instantly when global activities affect us.

Perhaps the age of blind acceptance is coming to a close. I presume many more people are asking questions these days. Growing up we would commonly get an answer like, "That's just the way things are." Nowadays if a child asks an adult a question and the adult doesn't know the answer, they are likely to pull out their cellular device and look it up on the spot. It's truly a great time to be alive, but the blessing comes with a curse. The mass amount of fingertip knowledge is accompanied by massive amounts of daily distraction and misinformation. What this overflow of information leads to is one half-truth after another. Rarely does one reach a substantial amount of corroborating evidence on the internet. The information is heavily biased. People still pick and choose what fits into their idea of truth without giving due justification or consideration to the other ideas. People will open the browser in search of the answer to one question and end up an hour later with a shopping cart full of miscellaneous nonsense.

We can believe in something in the sense that we feel that it is right, good, and true with little supporting evidence. Or, we can believe in something by putting our attention, our faith, and our trust in it routinely. In a sense we can start to believe and trust in things that are destructive, or coercive. Relying upon our technologies to the point that we turn nowhere else for information cuts us off from many things. We no longer have to use deductive reasoning, we can simply be told and answer. We no longer have to ask a friend or family member for advice we simply google it. We don't rely on natural sources for anything, we believe in, and have faith in computer technology. This emphasis on and reliance upon internet and computer tech has its place. However, in most cases it is severing our connection with the world around us. True, I can connect with those I have never seen, but it also causes us to stop seeing those in plain sight. We have become a society engrossed by the next new thing our "Phone" can do. A group of people sit down in a lobby and almost all of them will pull out their phone to stare at it. It takes us away from the here and now. It cuts us off from our families. It cuts us off from our daily tasks, our plans, and our goals.

The amount of time we invest in staring at our phones but accomplishing nothing is the testament of its purpose. So why am I still caught up on the whole phone/technology issue in the section about God? This book is designed to help you see things differently. What you believe in, what you have faith in, what you rely upon, what you think about, and the actions you take without question are determining the outcome of your life. If you are missing opportunities perhaps you were looking in the wrong direction. Instead of making an opportunity in that lobby full of strangers you pulled out your phone for distraction from the now in the precise moment you should have been paying attention. How can I see the opportunity in the moment when I believe my phone holds greater potential? The harder question is how do you loosen the noose as its cinching down tighter on your neck? Pull out your phone and google the answer or rely upon your own survival instincts? Obviously, you are a natural being. The more instinctual the answer the truer it will be for your life. As you syphon through the plethora of information you will gravitate towards things that have little meaning and substance. Our brains are wired up to a reward system. They are always looking for little hits of gratification. Try not to get caught up in all the mumbo jumbo intended on distracting you. Human being, you can either use tools or become one. Shield yourself once in a while. Take a technology fast. Make sure you have certain lengths of time where there is no technological distraction. Balance the computer life with real outdoor life. Most importantly would be to shield your children's exposure to computers, internet especially, and wireless devices. They are more susceptible to suggestion. They are still in early developmental stages which can have long lasting effects. How they process information and learn is being decided by the level of exposure they have to different stimuli. Also, the exposure to electromagnetic frequencies and pulses of radio waves may be detrimental to their health and wellbeing. I am not currently a medical doctor, nor am I trying to arouse fear, just elevating awareness. I am just suggesting that we be careful to not accept things as they are handed to us, but to inquire about them individually.

My concerns regarding technology and internet devices specifically stems from my own personal investigation. I began to see how it was changing my own perception. I could see how it was influencing my decisions. I noticed how it affected my social interactions. Simply seeing how magically it transmitted information I started to research its mechanical properties. I wondered how this advanced technology was so affordable and accessible while other simpler problems like hunger can't be changed. I thought, why am I enabled to have a super advanced pocket size computer, but am limited to driving a war influencing gas guzzler. All these questions led me to 1 answer. There's a new god in town. A new apple so to speak and were gobbling it up.

To be blunt, it's a trap. Beautifully and masterfully designed to capture your attention and time. At first glance you would assume that all this access to information was there for your benefit. You will think to yourself, "Wow, how empowering!" Most people now have a tool which can propel them forward in knowledge if used properly. It's human nature to get carried away in ideas. "What if" truly rules the undisciplined mind. Through the endless doors of this internet fantasy we get to experience the potential results of these, "what ifs". A true extension of our reality in a digital dimension. I implore you to keep your distractions to a minimum. If in fact you use this computer in your pocket properly it can create with you numerous opportunities for growth, advancement, and positive change. If you allow it to, it will become a controlling force in your life. This tool like your mind, has the power to build you up or tear you down. Choose wisely how you use it. Investigate the benefits, investigate the dangers. Do not just blindly accept it as necessary, passing it on to the next generation. It is our duty, before we pass on cultural and ideological norms, to thoroughly investigate them.

WHAT MASTERS DO YOU SERVE?

The purpose of this chapter is to approach our automatic belief system speculatively. I want the reader to recognize where in their own life they automatically believe, trust, and put their faith without personal analysis. Concentrating your mental energy on things that do not serve your highest purpose, in turn serves someone else's purpose. We are unique individuals. Each of us have personal contributions to make in this life. As we work towards defining our missions, we need to address the areas in life that are holding us back. To fulfill our purposes, we need to step out of the arena where we have been fulfilling others at the cost of our own.

Stages of life and the accompanying masters

1.) **Infancy** – The time from birth to about 2 years old. No self control, at the mercy of caretakers, vitality and development is dependent upon parent, guardian, state, and environment.

2.) **Early Childhood** – From 3 to 8 years old. These are the formative years. By approximately 7 this person has begun to solidify their reaction to environmental stimuli. Who we are and how we respond has been adopted and unconsciously carries on throughout life. Masters include parental figures, siblings, schooling, nutritional sources, religious establishments, and government.

3.) **Adolescence** – From about 9 to 18, but I would stretch it to about 23 as far as maturity is concerned. During this period, we begin to develop our "self". Our masters are the same as early childhood with the exception that we now have the liberty to control our own destiny. During this period, we will begin to make life altering choices, mastering ourselves though highly unconsciously.

4.) **Early Adulthood** – This is the period from about 19 to 45 years old. The most valuable of years in terms of personal development. We have become conscious that who we are is where we have been, and whom we have associated with. We now have the capacity to entirely control the outcome of our lives. Though we still will have masters to be aware of; family, partnership, business, nutrition, religion, and government will hold the power to determine our directions if we allow this to be so.

5.) **Middle Adulthood** – The period from 46 to about 65. Who we are is set in stone. By this stage we have developed habits and patterns that we are likely to never discard. We are the masters of our destiny, but still under controlling forces. All masters who we previously served, if they have not been deduced, and eradicated, will set the tone of our personal legacy.

6.) **Later Adulthood** – From 65+ years of age. We are who we are unapologetically. We should work diligently to ensure the best version of this character before it arrives. All masters solidified.

My scrutiny on our society and culture has to be rigorous. They say it takes a village to raise a child. Well we have all been raised and indoctrinated to the ways of the world through our respective local lenses. We are all brought up in a world of conformity. Either you fit in and do as you are told, or you're an outcast. You learn quickly what garners adulation and reproach. Over time we adopt customs and social norms simply as a measure of acceptance. Generally, our parents tell us who our God is, the school system teaches us to follow orders, and the real-world deals out heavy blows that insist our unquestionable toleration for the way it is. Nowhere throughout the process is one allowed or taught to think and act like an individual. We are expected to be a spoke in the wheel of a nonsensical machine. Until we see this and feel that call from inside to exemplify our individuality we will subconsciously conform to alternate truths. There are masters that we do serve, and then there are masters that we should serve. They all have the power to build us up or break us down and the choice is ours.

By the time you reach early adulthood or maturity you are serving several masters. Every facet of life calls for you to do its bidding. Most likely you are torn this way and that. Confused about which direction to travel. You are likely to be heading down several paths, none of them your own deliberate making. We become a product of circumstance and environment. This is the point in early adulthood where life drops us off like a tumbleweed. I know personally I have stood at many forks in the road only to continue the familiar path. This default choice is due to uncertainty, fear, misunderstanding, and my lack of knowledge of self. In this world it is easy to get caught up in pleasing others. We become paralyzed by the idea that we might let someone down. To protect their expectations for us we bury our own identity and serve life's ceaseless masters.

I'm using the term master in this section in an exaggerated sense, although I'm sure you understand. People, substances, habits, and ideas can easily dominate our lives. To me the most challenging part of life is the picking apart and separating that which is conducive to our highest self, from all that is detrimental. The challenge is in determining absolute bad or good. To that respect there is no such thing as absolute good or bad and so it complicates the issue.

As we go through this journey, we accumulate these aspects of polarity. Things that are good, to a degree are bad, and things that are bad, are to a degree good. When we come to love someone or something, we will find ourselves at times hating that very thing or person. That is because love and hate are the exact same emotion, just at polar opposites. As we get closer to the center of the spectrum the lines between love and hate mix into like and dislike. Over years our interpretation of this thing we love, or hate becomes discombobulated. The extremes of feelings we experienced create a web of deception and the subject of our "love" becomes a dominate force over which we have little to no control.

So, the main problem here is the polarity of our emotions, which is generally compounded with the ignorance we have of the emotion physiologically. By this I mean we have things in our life which we don't really know if they are good or bad, but we continue to drag them along for the ride. Why would I knowingly pollute and destroy my own body? Two reasons specifically; lack of information, and a lacking sense of personal value.

This part may seem like a bit of a downer, but I have to identify the problems to provide the solution. Here I will lay out a few of the masters we serve which may in fact be taking away from our lives potential and opportunity. Much of this might sound very controversial and contradicting to popular belief. I will do my best to explain how these things might rule over your life and divert you from your purposes without offense. Take note where you feel the most cognitive dissonance, these areas can be liberating.

INCOGNITO MASTERS

- ❖ **Money** – I'll start with one of the more obvious ones to ease you into this section. Most likely money has a very controlling force over your life. It has so many stigmas attached to it, "Money rules the world", "Money is the root of all evil", "Money makes the man", and so on. I am sure you can think of many more. My questions are; What are you doing for money, what personal sacrifices have you made in its name, what would you do with your life if money didn't exist?

  We can all relate to the stresses that money puts on our minds. I'm sure we have all done things to our bodies, working long hours, or some other physical pain to gain money. The issues money creates among friends and family can be life long. It is said that nothing is ever paid for with money, but the time of your life that it took to earn it.

Money is a concept, an idea created by man. It has no *real* value. This is a truth that holds up even without me delving into the illusory fiat currency we exchange daily. The only value money has is the emphasis we place on it collectively. Our entire monetary system is backed up on nothing of true value, no real asset, only an idea. The idea that we will keep on working and spending is all that keeps the economy afloat.

You might be thinking to yourself at this point it doesn't matter. Money makes the world go around and we have to use it. My point is to be that we not allow money to use us. Let us recognize what we truly value, let us see the real value of our lives, and let us begin to see the rat race were caught up in. Seeing money for what it is and recognizing the control it has over our lives is the first step in relinquishing its grasp.

❖ **Entertainment/ Technology** – I touched on the technology subject heavily early on in this chapter. I just wanted to include other forms of entertainment such as watching sports, to television shows, and music, etc. Basically, any form of entertainment where we are subjected to sights and sounds that are not created in nature. I know, I really sound like a fun hater. Look, were all on this life journey to figure it out for ourselves, you don't have to take my word on anything. This book is just to help anyone who wants to see things from a perspective we don't normally observe life from.

Regarding entertainment there are three things we don't commonly think about, but that have a significant controlling affect on our lives. The first thing is more obvious than the other, and that is the time we consume with these activities. When on the path to your truest self, time is of the essence. Secondly the words and images we absorb mold our concepts of reality. Thirdly, but closely tied to second is subliminal programming. Not only through the audio, and visual receptors, but directly to the brain through the ionosphere. Commercial advertising, and other propaganda is force fed to the human mind on a daily basis. These images, sounds, and radio-waves induce stress, and other chemical responses in our bodies which alter our behavior. Filtering what we put in as much as we can determines what we produce in return. This is also a perfect segue into the next master.

❖ **Food** – Food can easily become your master. It's quite paradoxical considering we need sustenance to survive. The problems with food are two-fold; ignorance and quality. Similar to thoughts, sounds, and images, the food we put in our bodies greatly affects our wellbeing. There are aspects of this topic that are blatantly obvious and others that are more controversial. First let's start with ignorance. It is our lack of understanding that transcends into issues such as addiction, over-indulgence, toxicity, and disease.

Generally speaking, the majority of people are not taught anything about food. I mean *real* food. We are not taught how to cultivate it, many are not taught how to prepare it for consumption, nor are we taught how the body assimilates the composites into energy. We have a few mandatory classes to graduate levels in school, but no real-world working knowledge is disseminated.

It is especially concerning in this day and time to become cognizant of our nutrition, it's origins, and functions. We must identify what we do not know about food and educate ourselves. Historically a person knew what they were eating, and it was from natural sources. In this modern time, you can actually 3D print "food".

This brings us to quality. What we consider now to be food is: *anything that is edible*. The ignorance we have about food in general is intimately tied to the second part of food being our master. Our food and nutrition have been and is continually being systematically designed to fuel economy not humanity. As a modern society in an industrialized nation, we do not know what the ingredients that make up our food are, or how they affect the body. The state of our diet has been evolving rapidly over the past century and a half. Science and business have intervened to genetically modify the seeds of our crops for mass production. Not only what is grown is modified, but how the products are processed, packaged, and sold has lost integrity. I'm just going to insert one of my favorite abbreviations here because we are all at different phases of the life cycle, and different points of perspective, (DYOR) Do Your Own Research.

The only chance one stands in feeding their body healthy, nutritious food, is self-education. We must investigate four ourselves what is good and what is bad. Also, we have to consciously choose to what degree we add these elements to our bodies. We could honestly devote our lives to learning about nutrition and how to apply the knowledge. The topic is that comprehensive and important.

❖ **Religion** – Obviously the elephant in the room would have to be mentioned eventually. I delayed it as long as I could. My society, culture, family, and friends will most critically analyze my opinion of this subject. If I am going to write what is authentic and true to my heart, then I can leave no stone unturned. At this point I could easily jump into my next subject, family, and highlight the powerful controlling influence it has on our decisions. I digress.

I want you to think for a second about writing a public critique on your natural born religion. For the vast majority it would be impossible without highlighting all the good and positive qualities. We all know there is good and bad in everything. The hammer that one uses to build, another uses to destroy. My objective is not to pick apart any religion. I only want to highlight how dominant and controlling of a factor this has on your life. For some people, their religion will determine the entire course of their life, they will have no choice whatsoever. For another, maybe the person runs from their religion and this result determines the outcome of their life. In both scenarios, their respective religions controlled their choices.

Are we drawn to or withdrawn from the tenets of our religion because of love or fear? In many cases we are evaluating our religion the entirety of our lives. We are uncertain because the facts presented to us as ignorant children come into question when we become logical young adults. So now we drag it along, scared to let go, and apprehensive to immerse ourselves absolutely. One foot in and one foot out.

On one side of the coin, the child in us fears being ostracized if we let it go. It fears damnation as punishment. The adult fears being childish in believing what could be potentially a fairytale. The adult has fears of eternal nothingness in death. The hope and promises of afterlife provided in a religion keeps it close to our hearts.

On the other side of the coin we can demonstrate our faith in human nature by believing. We are given abundant opportunities to spread love and healing. With our religion, the child in us is feels safe in an uncertain world. The adult can be admired for their strength in faith, and their apprehension of the religions' principles.

Who or what ever your God, The All, Brahman, Allah, Buddha, Christ, the Sun, or the Moon, we should seek fervently to understand why we believe in this omnipotence. Was it handed down to us in heredity and we accepted it without further inquiry? Have we done our own historical research and drawn our own conclusions? Are we damned if we do, and are we damned if we don't? That is the question. I will not assert that I have the answer on this personal quest. I do know this topic to be subjective, and the differing perspectives are all perfectly fine. My position is to make clear the path to opportunity. What we believe ultimately determines our path. Do we want the path of our creation? Do we co-create the path with our God? Should we follow a path that has been so heavily traversed? Or is that the sign where control is taking place? As we serve the masters of our life and come to understand the roles they play in our development, we cannot disregard who we call God for this is the most critical master.

❖ **Family** – I don't want the reader to misinterpret my position on family. I believe in the importance of family connections. Obviously, we can do nothing in this world if it were not for family. These people do not have to be biologically related although most of the time our life long comrades are. However tight knit or loosely woven your family is doesn't matter. What you should recognize is the lessons that you are meant to learn from each of these teachers.

I know we don't generally regard these people as teachers. In some cases, we will have built deep seated resentments and animosity towards a family member. We can easily get to a point where we distance ourselves from them and think of how separate we are, "I'm not like them", or "I could never learn anything from someone like that." There is an immense pool of learning and growth potential hidden in the worst of these family relationships. This is just one important aspect of family to keep in mind. The power that one of these sour relationships can have to mold your entire perspective on life should be recognized.

Secondly the good relationships hold just as much power in controlling our lives. In the good relationships we all want what's best for each other. Or so we think. We want what's best for ourselves. So, the loving concern and opinion of an endeared family member has significant bearing on your choices.

The teachers are there for guidance and advice until we can accurately make decisions for our lives as individuals. We need people with more wisdom then us throughout life. Though there comes a point when you should be relying on your own intuition, inspiration, and unique dreams. After you reach a certain age, mentality, or maturity level in life you should value your own decision higher than someone else's opinion for your life. I'm not saying to disregard others' perspectives, just that there is a point we must trust our own inner voice more. What is true for one is not always true for another.

Going against family values, traditions, and expectations posits us against the most unforgiving masters. We can easily remain life long servants to outdated idols or customs which no longer serve us in this journey. Being able to define your life how you deem fit gives it the highest value that you can attain. It may cost you important relationships, but if the other person is opposed to your choice for your life, their interpretation of true love is distorted. When we don't like someone else's decision it's because we are more concerned how it will affect us then how they feel about it. This area and the topics can get shadowy. Keep in mind that the choices we make at this point should be to our highest benefit, or vision for ourselves. If the choices are detrimental to your health, the lively hood of others, and family is concerned, they are then afforded the critique of your lifestyle. So long as that decision for your life is not interfering with the health, peace, or prosperity of life it is perfectly fine. Remember that they are there for you to learn and grow to become your best self. Sometimes they will be the only factors that align you in the proper track.

❖ **Alcohol & Drugs** – Everyone is aware to some degree about the nature of these substances. We know about the addictive tendencies and harmful properties involved with indulging in these products. Some of these substances may in fact hold medicinal elements and contribute positively to your life. However, the overwhelming emphasis on these products is in what they take away from you, not what they give.

I'm not writing this section to debate the benefits vs. adverse effects. I'm writing to highlight what it takes to embody your highest self possible. Whether you have used or abused these substances doesn't matter. As I've said over and over, all things in this world have a place for your personal growth. There are lessons to be learned from these substances for the student who needs the lesson.

Don't get caught in the *trap*. Much easier said than done. To be as specific and concise as possible I'll call it for what it is. Few who enter the maze ever make it to the true high ground. As with all other things in this life, synthetic drugs, alcohol, natural, and chemical substances can become dominating aspects on your course. Very easy to get swept in, and very hard to find your way out. The whole system is designed to keep you trapped once you enter, but this will be considered conspiracy until you can truly see.

The facts remain, many of these addictive concoctions are promoted as healthy and good in our societies. They are often glamorized as part of the most ideal lifestyle. These elements are destructive to the body in all areas, but most importantly cognitive functions. Once swept up and adopted as part of a lifestyle, they can direct the remaining course of your life, even if your true self disapproves of your actions. This is a sad and dangerous reality. The only fighting chance you have of making it out, and back to consciously directing your life, is that inner voice. The one that calls and guides. It says this is not good for me. It knows, you know, and that is the only chance you have of escaping the grips of self destruction. The ultimate objective is consciousness. To be awake, to be aware fully. That is how we capitalize on opportunity. Diluting our mind dilutes the moment. When all we have is the "NOW" it is best to be present in mind and body.

You know, I've prayed my entire life. It turns out we pray way more than we realize. Information comes in and our thoughts go out. For the longest time I never really knew who or what was listening. My family and culture taught me that I was praying to God or Jesus. I could never fully grasp that concept until now. It just made no sense to me how God could hear my thoughts, but I was instilled with this belief. It was something I was taught. Even though I couldn't comprehend the mechanics of it, I believed that it was true.

Throughout the world, all cultures of people rely on a form of prayer. We dance for the God's, chant for them, meditate, sing, sacrifice, and pray. Even though we may not understand why, we believe we are communicating to our creator, and this is our universal truth. I'm certain even those among us who do not believe in God find themselves talking to It from time to time. They probably catch themselves mid sentence and laugh, "Ah, who am I talking to?" Well I will tell you it is certainly not only yourself who you are talking to.

Either you can believe through faith or you can believe through empirical evidence. Your body and mind send and receive information likened to an organic antenna. Mountains of evidence supports this truth. You don't even have to utter a word and someone in the same room as you can pick up on your thought. Out loud they will say the words in your head. When you come to understand the power of this transmitting potential, you will recognize too the power of prayer.

Whether we want it or not we need this truth. We are endowed with this capability for the same reason one is endowed with the tools for procreation. It is fundamental to our existence and survival. To believe in yourself fully, you must know that you are connected to your source. This knowledge will give you strength and confidence in yourself. It will help you see through the darkest of clouds this life brings.

I didn't know who I was praying to. In fact, many times in life I doubted anyone, or anything was listening. I even denounced God in hopes that I could insight a sign of some sort, even if it was a vengeful sign. I wanted proof and felt like I didn't have any. Deep down I hoped that someone was listening. As it turns out for me, I just didn't know what I was looking for.

For instance, I want to take you back to chapter one. The story of my careless and reckless driving that turned out to alter my life. I want you to know that I prayed for a long time. Many years I prayed for a way out of that lifestyle. Many signs were posted saying, "This way out". I was too caught up serving other masters. Blinded by my lifestyle, circumstances, peers, personal motives, and societal obligations to see those opportunities. One day the prayers were answered, and a door was busted wide opened. Just as easily as I could walk through that door and begin transforming my life, I can easily loose sight and walk back out. You can lead a horse to water as they say, but you can't make it drink. The last thing I want you to know about this is that the farther away from misinformation, distractions, and calamity, the more doors I see ready to swing open.

CHAPTER 5

RECLAIMING LIFE

I suspect there comes a time in everyone's life when they want to relinquish the demands and expectations held to them. I'm sure at one point or another we will each think to ourselves, "I want to do what I want for a change." For some people this natural impulse is stronger. Some people are born to be "caretakers". They spend their entire lives willfully to the call of others. Either way, even they too will reach the point, "What about me?" I say, "Yes, what about you?" What do you want? What do you believe? What have you buried and pushed aside? Why are you here? If not now, when?

There is nobility in selfless acts. There is righteousness in the paths of service to others. Your good works do not go unaccounted for. They add a positive balance to the checkbook of your life. In order to truly be of great service to the world you must be doing what you incarnated to do. To get to this point we have to be a little self-seeking. It's not a bad thing. This is our life and our time to do with it what we will. Finding yourself allows you to be that unique expression the world needs. Perhaps you have had a sense of your calling deep inside. Maybe you have silenced it, or the world silenced it for you to the point it isn't recognizable anymore. Maybe you have not yet learned what your calling is. They say, "When the student is ready, the master will appear." It's my job, and others along your path, to facilitate in the cultivation of your true self. We must focus our energy and attention on ourselves for weeks, months, and even years until we forge a true path.

Let's take for example my passion and concern for the homeless. I don't waste my time with why they are homeless in the face of despair. Someone might say, "Well, he got himself in this situation." Although this statement is true, my beliefs, and understanding of natural laws afford me the compassion and empathy. I cannot turn a blind eye and disregard someone for the poor choices they have made. We all go through life making uninformed or misinformed choices. We all make mistakes, the least among us is as deserving as the best among us. Maybe this specific person never had someone who cared for them. Maybe they sacrificed everything for what they thought was the greater good, only to end up with nothing in the end. Maybe they chose to commit crime, steal, harm, and take from everyone they encountered. My point to this story is not about judging a book by its cover, but about writing one entirely.

I can go out right now and give the token homeless person enough money to get a room for the night. That would seemingly be the right course of action. Or, let's say I just go through life without finding my purpose and just give the homeless people 5 bucks here and there. I could feel good about myself that day and maybe it would lift their spirits for a minute. Throughout my time here I have done just that. Random acts of kindness. These are good to do, but in a way leave me feeling empty as if I did nothing at all for them. Luckily, I learned a very important lesson in life about the wellspring of opportunity which surrounds us. Instead of giving 1 person a room for the night, or 5 bucks for a meal, I am empowered with the capacity to insight real change. I set out to use the power of language and words which was freely given to me. From the point of this publication on I will carry copies with me everywhere I travel and give them to those I see on the corners. They can then be reminded through this literature that they aren't in need of a few bucks, but a renewal of perspective.

I couldn't and wouldn't have written this book or any other if I had not been self-seeking. I realized that if I did not focus on myself for a long period of time, I could not become who I was meant to be. We need to be introspective. We need to cherish our dreams. We need to discover our callings. We need to develop ourselves. We need to command our directions and master our missions. It's ok to want what you want, just make sure that it is the true YOU that wants it. To help with the process of reclaiming your true identity. Here are the places, points, and aspects of the conditioned self that should be nurtured.

Process of Mastery

This process is to be used in conjunction with the *5 keys for a harmonic life.* The keys help unlock the cages of captivity releasing you from your former self to fulfill your highest purpose. The process of mastery is as follows; Dream, Discover, Develop, Command, and Master. What I'm referring to when I said "Cage" is the mental barriers in between what you want and what you have, what you are and what you can be, and where you've been and where you are going. Let's get started.

The first part of the process is **Dream**. I don't mean in the sense of going to sleep and hitting REM stage, although that is important for your wellbeing. I'm talking about what did you want to be when you were growing up? Or, what major vision did you have for your life? What do you feel at this point in your life is the most important, but seemingly impossible to accomplish? If you had all the time and resources what would you dedicate your life to? Money is not an issue, time is not an issue, now think what your life's work would be.

Now you have to separate the ego self from the true self. The ego self will have created a world for you in your imagination, and your authentic self will have created a vision for you as well. These two ideas generally conflict in interest unless you are on course already. The ego tells you to pursue this calling for money, fame, security, glory, and vanity. Your authentic calling will draw your attention to more profound or simpler matters that highlight stress free or low stress, natural abilities, intuitive drives, humanitarian efforts, new ideas, and creative work.

The cages of captivity surrounding our dreams are comprised of many forms and features. However, they all hide behind the same mask, *FEAR*! Examples of cages; I'm not good enough, I'm too old/young, that idea is too risky, I don't have the skills, it's too expensive, I'm too this or that, I don't have the time.

(*Take a moment and jot down some dreams that you have had for your life. Use your intuition, the guiding voice that says this choice is right and good.*)

Now revisit the list of dreams and jot down some of your own personal cages of captivity. What are the things that have stopped you from pursuing your dreams? What are your roadblocks from opportunity? Once you have your dreams laid out, and you can see what stood in your way, its time to figure out why. Why are the obstacles in your way and why is it worth overcoming?

This part of the process is **Discovery**. Here we find out how to begin implementing our dreams or making them a reality. The first thing you must grasp is that whatever you can conceive, you can achieve. I know this sounds cliché, but everything that is was once just a thought. In the discovery process we need to uncover. We need to discover what dream we want to pursue exactly. We need to identify the cages we can get through alone, and which ones will require assistance. We will find out when we overcome them, who we really are. Your problems are personal, but someone out there has been in your shoes. Mentors don't have to be someone you have met personally, there are abundant resources and materials to cater to your dilemma.

Discovering the whys are easier said than done. I'm not going to sugar coat it. Following your life's missions are very trying. Looking ourselves in the eyes is a challenge few are willing to take. Though, once we realize that we alone are our only obstacle, the process gets easier and begins to flow naturally. We will begin to discover that 99% of the cages of captivity are self-imposed. The 1% of your limitations that didn't come directly from your own mind can be transmuted or at least comprehended. This now leaving us with 100% accountability and possibility. When we take the time to discover what we placed in our own way and follow the rabbit hole the problems unravel. We start to catch ourselves and stop blockages in the process. Relieving our life from sabotage. The weight of half a lifetime can shed from your shoulders instantly. Courage, pride, and honor replace fear and trepidation.

1% cages would consist of things like; cultural conditioning, physical impairments, existential circumstances beyond our direct control.

As you work on the process of reclamation keep in mind and apply the 5 keys for a harmonic life. The keys go hand in hand with this process. So, you will want to pay attention to your intuition with the first part dealing with your dreams. In the part on discovery you will want to employ motivation.

You should think positive, look at things from a different perspective, gather insight, formulate ideas, brainstorm, write, and begin planning. Stay motivated and begin to look at ways to make your ideal life a reality. Establish your goals at this point. Begin to visualize your concept of the new reality. Dismantle obstructive thoughts mentally. The discovery part should set in stone for you a new path and way of life. Don't be afraid to live your life, it's yours. Following what we have discovered about ourselves thus far we will move on to the next stage of the process, **Development**.

What do you truly believe in? Somewhere very near, if not at the absolute top should be the answer, "Myself". In order to develop along the path of your highest calling you need 2 things; 1 a strong, convicted belief in yourself, and 2 information for empowerment. Without one or the other of these elements, the development will be uneven and insufficient.

Here's why those two things are the most important, when it comes to developing your new self. In this life, your life, it is imperative that you refine your character. The entire life process is designed for growth and change. Either you can consciously make the changes necessary or life will change you on its own. Believing in yourself is the catalyst for manifesting your destiny.

If I was to continue as I was years ago, just wandering through life with no definite purpose and no knowledge of self, I would have become a useless byproduct of the world. This is how people get caught up in the thinking that this whole life is random and accidental. To the untrained eye everything appears to be haphazard. However, after proper thought cultivation and training your perception properly, you begin to see the order. I touched on this in earlier chapters, so I want to get back to self-confidence at the moment.

You will either get this point right now, sometime before the end, or in the final moments of your life, you are here on purpose. Once you recognize this fact you will feel empowered knowing that there is a reason for all of this. If you see life as a challenge, or something stressful, realize it is only how you feel about it, and not how it is. Work the processes in this book and you will gradually begin to see the opportunities, ease, and flow of life. Knowing you have a purpose will give you the self-assuredness to find out exactly what the purposes are. Sometimes you have to look for it like lost keys. You know you had them moments ago. Keep searching, those keys you lost are in plain sight.

Having a purpose, you need to believe you have the capacity to fulfill it. This part can be hard, and life will show up to give you many challenges. Refinement or reclamation of self is a process of endurance. Things are not always easy, but if you see your challenges for what they are, then you can laugh at the universe when they appear. I call the cages of the developmental stage as "setbacks". We all know what a set back is. We deal with them all throughout life. When they show up during the process of reclaiming your life and purpose, just know that they are there to help you mold a certain area in a specific way. More often than not the set back is to teach you to look at something a different way than you are accustomed to.

This is where information plays an integral role in your development. In this part of the process we can't just continue down the old path and think were on a new one because we've made a few positive changes here and there. The transformation picks up its momentum through self-education. There's work to be done. You have to learn to unlearn that which is not true for your life. You have been taught many things, assumingly righteous and true. Thoroughly re-inspect your belief system and pick it apart carefully. Books, videos, audios, speeches, and people will enter your life now with precise timing. This go around you can recognize it is for a reason. Do not overlook these as meaningless coincidences, they are part of your journey and showing up right on time. Trust the process.

It is a living process. By the time you get to the fourth stage, **commanding**, all previous elements will be active and well on their way to transforming your life. You will be holding on to your dream, listening to intuition, staying motivated, continuing to discover new things, informing yourself, and developing.

Now you are using the action key and all of its potential commanding your life. No longer do we tumble when the wind blows, we adjust our sails. We have finally taken control of the vessel and demanded certain distinct results.

We thought we were in control before all of this, and to a degree we were. Well in fact we were entirely, but it has mostly been unconscious and the results lack luster. Before we controlled our thoughts and emotions, the world appeared cold and brutal. Now we can see that it was just our interpretation and our attitude towards circumstance that made it cold.

Commanding our life and demanding specific results requires a ton of action on our part. Before I learned all of this, I thought I was acting and performing well in life. I would wake myself up on time, drive to work, break my back for whatever company I was working for, come home, be there for my family, etc. Only now do I realize that automatic process was me existing to be used as a means to someone else's ends. I wasn't doing anything I truly wanted or believed in. I was caught in a trap watching my life dwindle away.

As you advance to this stage of the process you have to stay alert. The most important part is keeping your mind sharp. You have to be privy to the ways of this world. The cages of captivity may be subtler at this point, more inconspicuous, and harder to detect. Distraction and complacency are the two sneakiest cages at this point. They will try to make you fall back on your old way of life. Distraction will take you away from your duties, responsibilities, and true purposes. Complacency will try to convince you that your pursuits are not worthwhile. That the hill is just to steep, resting here would be a better idea than continuing to climb. Keep your guard high on these two and you can advance to the next stage.

We are all born to be masters of our destinies, admirals of navigation through the sea of life. The final stage of reclaiming your original self is **mastery**. Whether your life mission involves a craft, or a service, whatever it may be, mastery should be the ultimate goal. We want to set our bench marks as high as possible to master this life. For some this comes naturally, and we see them advance past us effortlessly. Some are born so inclined as to be deemed genius or prodigy becoming masters at a young age. On the other hand, most people would be lucky to ever master anything.

The highest level of mastery is not over a craft, or a field of work, but over the self. Conquering your "demons" and learning to control your mind and body is the highest form of flattery to your creator. Honoring your body and mind to a point where your discipline preserves it in every way is the greatest achievement a person can make in this world. It is my opinion, and the opinion of many masters, as written in the texts around the world, that conquering self is the objective of this life.

Whether you conquer yourself entirely or not, just reclaiming your dreams, and pursuing the life you choose is of very high and distinguished value. Mastering a craft, service, or trade that you believe in would define your purpose in a remarkable way. To live intentionally and direct your course to these ends will make it all worthwhile.

The time is now! I hope that you have been taking notes throughout this book. The power of words is unyielding. When I began the journey of reclaiming my life, I didn't have an instruction manual. I didn't know all the things I know now about the universal laws. I felt my way through the process and am still going strong. There have been many challenges, the majority of them are mental, and of my own creation. I had to find the real me which was drastically different than the one I had been creating for years.

I decided to write this book upon a profound revelation. Everything is opportunity. One day I was cleaning up the garage in July of 2016. I was thinking to myself how I could make some money that day. Being newly self-employed as an artist, I didn't always have customers to buy my art. I really put the starving in the term starving artist, but I digress. Being so crafty and good with my hands I was thinking of alternatives to painting that day. Maybe some type of constructive work or demolition perhaps. Looking around the garage I gazed upon a hammer and had this feeling come over me of lightness. I just felt joy and laughter from deep inside. Every trouble seemed so insignificant at that moment. I realized that everything in this world is just opportunity and nothing less. It's all just endless possibilities. The hammer was not just a hammer, but an incredibly simple tool of empowerment. Imagine all that one could create with the use of a hammer. I began looking around at everything and smiling in bewilderment. All this time I felt so closed off to opportunity yet everything I looked at had the potential to change my life.

With the proper dedication, vision, information, and action I could take that hammer and become a master builder if I willed it so. This idea might seem out there, but I challenge you. Show me 1 thing in this entire world that is not opportunity in some shape or form. A blade of grass is opportunity for a caterpillar to eat. A grain of sand holds innumerable life lessons to be taught. Anything and everything is opportunity. It is all just a matter of perspective. Grasp this fact and watch as all closed doors before you fly open.

Thank you for reading, I'm humbled to be a part of your journey.

Shane L. Freeman

In order to see that everything is opportunity, a person must remove the obstructions from their view. There is a saying I heard at a meeting one time it's profound truth and simplicity stuck with me, "You can't see the forest from the trees." This means you cannot step outside your own frame of reference. When you're in the forest you can't see the immensity of your problem. You cannot see how deep and how far the trees stretch casting endless shadows. To see where you are clearly you have to change your perspective and start to think differently.

All of that said to get to this point. Who or what do you fear? In what ways are you holding yourself back? What is unworthy of your time and energy? What is controlling you? These and many more are very real questions we should be asking ourselves. It's ok to be self seeking at times. If you do not cater to your own interests and abilities, you will push your true purpose to the side and live a life fulfilling someone else's. By fulfilling our purposes as individuals, we are contributing to the collective.

Believing in yourself can sometimes be the hardest challenge in life. The world tries to give us so many reasons not to. We try, we fail, and become discouraged. Others reinforce our own self judgment with their opinions. Maybe we have felt less than worthy. I know that I have certainly reached points in life where I just felt like giving up. I just didn't know how to get things right. It seemed that no matter what I did I always ended up broke and empty. To top it all off I would earnestly pray for a reprieve, which more often then not went seemingly unanswered. The fact of the matter was I just couldn't see. I was detached, disconnected. We will have times like this. But the universe will always try to pull you back to where you belong. Tap into the unending potential within yourself and your surroundings to find your way back home. Always remember, Everything is Opportunity!

Printed in Great Britain
by Amazon

74222014R00076